D1580956

Journey to the Unknown: 1982, HMS Hermes

George McDonald

2019

Dedication

To all those still on patrol and will never be forgotten
RIP

Especially David Lee, SMR H.M.S. Glamorgan Flt.
Alan MacCauly, SMR H.M.S. Ardent Flt.

Acknowledgements

To my team on board, H.M.S. Hermes, Air Engineering Department, covering, aircraft ground equipment, motor transport, which included all the flight deck tractors, aircraft salvage crane, forklifts, mechanical handlers, ships landrovers, also the aircraft fuelling points, in the hangar and around the flight deck, including the aircraft ground electrical points.

Without this team my job would have been impossible. They were loyal and hard working 24 hours a day and I would like to take this opportunity to thank them for their support, also for looking after each other during those difficult times.

Contents

Medals: *South Atlantic medal, + Long service and good conduct medal.*

CHAPTER ONE

Early Days

~ • ~

Who am I? My name is George McDonald and I was born on 28 Feb 1946 in the Sick Children's Hospital in Edinburgh, Scotland.

I am the youngest of six and the younger of twins. My sister Jean popped out 20 minutes before me. She must have taken all the goodness while inside because I spent the first six weeks in an incubator before being let out on my own!

My parents, Jimmy and Peggy, passed away many years ago now.

We lived in a happy home; not much money but we were certainly a happy family with lots of laughter, which, being from Scotland, was the norm, and still is.

I attended infant school from age 5 to 7 years, where I first experienced corporal punishment – the strap – which I was to find out was going to be something that was going to be a regular occurrence throughout my school life for things like being late, talking in class, not doing my homework, and pinching the girls' balls or skipping ropes. I even got the strap once for finishing an exam first! Another time was for being late after attending to my sick pigeon.

As I was reaching my 15th birthday, I decided that I wanted to see the world and that, if I joined the Royal Navy and went to sea, my mum wouldn't have so much ironing, etc., to do, so I went to the Royal Navy recruiting office in George Street, Edinburgh, and sat the entrance test.

I used to get free school meals, but on a Friday night we always had a 'fry-up' at home; usually bacon grill, egg and beans. It was lovely. One Friday night during teatime, my dad said, "I have a job for you. You do your apprenticeship at Swanston garage in Colinton, then afterwards join Smiths of Leith as a diesel fitter." I said that I didn't want to do that.

The following Friday he again said, "I've got you a job. You go to the riding stables at Haddington and become an apprentice jockey (I was only 5 feet 2 and a quarter inches tall and less than 8 stone and I used to help in the stables across the road from our house at Colinton Main Green). I told him that I had joined the Navy. There was silence, but when the time came my parents signed the necessary papers.

I had sat my final exams at school, Tyncastle School next to the Heart of Midlothian Football Club ground and passed my Edinburgh School Leaving Certificate on 9 March 1961. I was in class when I was told that I was required in the Headmaster's office. As I entered the office, I noticed that there was a Royal Navy officer there along with a Chief Petty Officer (CPO). This is when I realised that my school days were going to be over. The CPO said that someone had dropped out of the following week's recruitment into the Navy and would I take his place? So, I said that I would, now knowing that the break between school and work was no longer going to take place.

I was now 15 years and 9 days old. I can't remember what was going through my mind over the weekend; I just knew that, as the weekend passed, the more I was regretting what I was doing (but I didn't want anyone to know).

It was arranged that, when I left, my brother-in-law, David, would give me a lift to Waverley Station in his van. On the Monday, after saying my goodbyes, I climbed into the van. Deep down inside I was hoping that Dave would get to the station late so that I would miss my train, but all he kept saying was, "Don't worry, we'll get there on time." And we did.

The train was to take me to the recruiting office in Glasgow, for my final medical, where I was given a long glass jar by the doctor and told, "I need a urine sample." I stared back at the doctor, and so he said, "Piss in the jar!" Thinking that you got medals for everything, I thought that if I filled this jar up I'd get one! Imagine that! Going home with a medal and your family and friends asking, "What did you get the medal for? Pissing in a bottle? You must be brave!"

So, the jar was full to the brim but **no** medal!

After the medical, I was introduced to the other lads – all a bit older than me but under 16 years of age.

That evening, we were all put on the overnight train to England; never having been to a 'foreign' country before. We got to our destination, Ipswich, where we got the bus to Shotley, got off the bus and walked through the gates of the annex to HMS *Ganges*, the Royal Navy's boys training school. I was now starting a 25-year career in the Royal Navy as an aircraft engineer at the ripe-old age of 15 years and 13 days.

CHAPTER TWO

Prior to Departure, March/April 1982

~ • ~

A ll leave cancelled in order to store ship. In Portsmouth, on the quayside by the ship, I counted more than 40 articulated lorries of all different sizes; some military, with spare parts for the ship and its aircraft, stores, etc.

One of the vehicles was a mobile aircraft repair and transport salvage unit (MARTSU); my previous draft before joining the *Hermes*. The driver was a Mr Norman Thorpe, who was a Ministry of Defence civilian driver, an ex-Royal Navy seaman with many a story to tell. We were good friends and had transported many a helicopter by road throughout the UK.

When I saw that it was Norman, once his lorry had been unloaded, I took him to the mess for a couple of refreshing drinks. Afterwards, he made his way down the gangway to drive his lorry back to HMS *Daedalus*, at Lee-on-Solent, MARTSU's headquarters, but was stopped on the gangway by the Joss (master at arms and head of discipline on the ship); not for being drunk but because all leave was cancelled. The Joss didn't believe Norman when he said that he wasn't part of the crew, so I had to go over to explain!

To unload the lorries, there was a human chain made up of crew members (this was the normal procedure for storing ships in the Royal Navy), handing boxes from one person to the next, snaking up the gangway and into the darkness of the labyrinth of passageways throughout the ship. All items are stored in their allocated places. This time, we were taking on more than the usual stores because some were destined for the ships that were on their way home from foreign deployment but were now getting rerouted to the South Atlantic, so stores allocated for them were being shipped by the *Hermes*. Boxes, crates and bags of vegetables were stored in the passageways throughout the ship.

Some ships that were on their way home from Middle or Far East deployment were ordered into the Gibraltar dockyard to have the ship stored again, including with ammunitions. On completion, they sailed away, leaving Gib on the horizon. Once through the Straits of Gibraltar, they turned left instead of right to go home. They were now on their way to the South Atlantic. I believe that Admiral Sandy Woodward was on one of these ships and later transferred with his team on to HMS *Hermes*, making *Hermes* the flagship for the South Atlantic Task Force.

But back to Portsmouth, where the preparing of the *Hermes* was now in full swing. The larger items were craned onboard either by the dockyard crane, the ship's crane, or the Coles crane: a 14-ton crane usually used for aircraft salvage (its main purpose) on the flight deck. But today it was being used for a more important task: hoisting barrels of beer onboard for the senior rates mess (which was my mess. Sometimes, priorities have to be changed!).

Eventually, all the lorries had been unloaded and everything stored away, knowing that the same was going to happen the next day and the day after that until it was time to sail; every minute was required to store ship. On completion of the day's tasks, the 'pipe' came that shore leave was now permitted. I got ready and went ashore for a couple of beers, meeting up with an old friend, who was my next-door neighbour. While ashore, I took the opportunity to make some telephone calls to family and friends. The conversations were very vague due to the secrecy of what we were doing and where we were going, although I think that everybody

Part of the MT Fuel and Salvage team, 1982.

knew what was going on because it had been publicised and reported on the news.

The ship had just returned from a trip, long enough for it to be transformed from a fighting unit, where everything and everyone was operating like clockwork, to a different kind of activity, that only occurs when a ship enters into the dockyard for its routine refit and repairs. The ship was empty of all its aircraft; these aircraft having flown ashore to their respective parent air stations. The Sea Harriers of its 800 Squadron had disembarked to the Royal Naval Air Station Yeovil: HMS *Heron*. The Sea King helicopters of 826 Squadron had disembarked to the Royal Naval Air Station Culdrose: HMS *Seahawk*. When the squadrons disembarked, they took with them all their equipment and manpower, leaving the ship with a reduced crew of about 1,000 personnel, which was good for the remainder of us because we had more space around the ship and in the messes and cabins.

The reason why squadrons disembark is so that aircrew and personnel can keep flying and training so they are always ready for anything that is thrown at them, keeping them in tip-top condition and readiness to protect their ship, etc., carrying out the tasks and operations that is required of them.

As I mentioned earlier, like the aircraft, the ship required its routine service and rectification of repairs and also any modifications, which, for a ship the size of *Hermes* was a mammoth task and therefore we were in Portsmouth on refit. The majority of the manpower was now dockyard personnel, in their green overalls, moving around the ship like a rash. I'm sure a good percentage of them walked around all day doing as little as possible – which they weren't aware was about to change – their portable toolboxes and machinery were laying around the ship everywhere.

I remember when we sailed on sea trials after the ramp on the flight deck had been installed for the operation of the Sea Harrier aircraft, some of the dockyard personnel sailed with us for the five-day sea trials. On returning to Portsmouth, after they had left the ship, we noticed that all the 'nicks' and socks that should have been drying in the bathroom areas had gone missing!

The flight deck was now cluttered; non-recognisable. It was covered with all the equipment required for the tasks to be carried out. A right mess! Green overalls moving around here, there and everywhere. I think I did see someone working, although it might have been an illusion! The 'island' that would be standing proud on the starboard side of the flight deck was now covered in scaffolding, which looked like a giant cobweb, with lots of spiders moving and climbing all over it wearing their green overalls.

The island housed the ship's bridge, flying operations controlled from here (Flyco), aircrew refreshments (ACRB) and the aircraft control room (ACR), from where the aircraft not flying were controlled, whether in the hangar or on the flight deck. High up within the island you would also find the communications room and the Met room.

Just inside the island access, next to the ACR, also where the pilots signed for and accepted their aircraft, was a double ladder going down into the ship, which gave access to a small town, which lay underneath the flight deck and hangar. It had everything required to bring the ship alive for fighting, celebrating, sleeping, eating, entertaining and cooking, as well as a hospital, workshops, hangar, stores and administration. There was also a Chinese laundry, and the dining rooms would double up as the cinema. Next to the hangar side lift was one of the most important rooms on the ship, which was my project: MacMo's ice cream parlour, which I ran when I was not working (more about this later). Underneath all these were the engine rooms and boiler rooms. At that time, the ship's company did not know what lay ahead of them and that everything and everyone would be stretched to their limits and beyond: personnel and equipment coming and going, including sailors, soldiers, marines, Special Boat Service (SBS), Special Air Service (SAS), not forgetting the RAF chappies. You name it and at least one of these groups would be onboard *Hermes* during the next six months.

The ship the *Hermes* was laid down on 21 June 1944 and launched on 16 February 1953. She was eventually commissioned on 25 November 1959 as a fixed-wing aircraft carrier of the Centaur class, of around 24,000 tons. I was fortunate enough to serve on the ship as a naval air mechanic (airframe and engines) from 1965 to 1967 with 849B Flight, of which the aircraft were Fairey Gannets Mk3; aircraft early warning. We had three aircraft plus a COD Gannet, used for delivering and collecting mail and also to fly persons ashore on compassionate grounds. The ship also carried six Mk2 Blackburn Buccaneers. This was the last type of military aircraft completely built in the UK and belonging to 809 Naval Air Squadron. Then there were: six Mk2 Sea Vixen aircraft belonging to 892 Naval Air Squadron; the helicopters, belonging to 826 Naval Air Squadron; six Sea King aircraft used for anti-submarine detection (Pinger Squadron) and three Wessex Mk1 helicopters used for search and rescue. These were also used as plane guards, flying alongside the ship at flight deck level during aircraft launch and recovery. In case of an incident where an aircraft ended up in the water, they were already airborne ready

Tea time at Mill.

to assist. The fixed-wing aircraft were launched by steam catapult (a British invention) and recovered by arrester wires across the aft part of the flight deck. There were usually four or five of these (another British invention).

So, the period from January 1981 through to April 1983 was my second commission on the 'Happy Hermes', as she was affectionately known. Apparently, she was also known as the 'Homo Hermes' because she always reversed into the dockyard!

Hermes was the 10th Royal Navy ship to be named Hermes. Her battle honours were as follows: 1852 Burma; 1940 Atlantic; and 1982 Falkland Islands.

During the 1960s and during my time onboard with 849B Flight, we were deployed east of Suez (transiting the Suez Canal), steaming around the Aden area for six weeks to assist with and cover the withdrawal of the British troops from Aden in 1967, when the famous Army officer called Mad Mitch was in overall charge there. We were to return to our anchorage at Aden, just off HMS *Sheba* on the Friday. During the weekend, several of the duty personnel would be detailed off, to go ashore by ship's boats in order to assist the army in patrolling the area. Then it would be back onboard and, after the weekend, the ship would sail back out into the

Indian Ocean or into the Red Sea areas. Our aircraft would then fly over the Aden area to let the locals know that we were still there. I believe that HMS *Victorious* was also there at the same time.

I was selected twice to go ashore. On one occasion, another air mechanic and I were detailed off to patrol the officers' beach area. It was very quiet, so we stripped off and went for a swim. If anything had happened we could really do nothing because, although we had a .303 rifle, we had no ammunition. If we required any, we were to blow our whistle and someone would bring a bullet! In the Royal Navy they say that the most dangerous thing on the planet is a matelot with a gun!

But back to 1982.

We had been in Portsmouth now for two or three weeks and the ship's refit was going well. Once again, green overalls everywhere. Sometimes you saw them moving or maybe working! My own department was responsible for aircraft fuel delivery and aircraft salvage, which I had experience of from RNAS *Portland* and MARTSU, covering five years of aircraft salvage and recovery. The department also included: the helicopter inflight refuelling rig (HIFR); the aircraft ground equipment, which included the aircraft jacking equipment; oil and hydraulic replenishing rigs; hydraulic system test rigs; all the motor transport onboard, which included four ship's Land Rovers (one lovely blue one for the Skipper's use); six all-wheel drive and all-wheel steer flight deck tractors for moving the aircraft around the flight deck; two JCB telescopic forklifts; two other forklifts: four electrical mechanical handlers for moving the aircraft in the hangar; and one 14-ton Coles crane, whose main purpose was aircraft salvage on the flight deck; **not** lifting the pallets of beer onboard, although it was used more times for doing that task than its main task! If there was an incident, the crane would be required to lift the aircraft clear if it was obstructing the deck in any way (only required once, but I'll come back to that later).

Now, all the vehicles were ashore being serviced by POST(N) garage for servicing and the repairs that were required before going back to sea. The Land Rovers were kept at the bottom of the gangway so that they were available for the ship's crew to use on a controlled basis. Of course, the lovely blue one with white upholstery was for the Skipper's (Captain Linley Middleton) use only. (He was a lovely man and a gentleman; unfortunately, no longer with us. RIP, Sir.) He never drove the Land Rover himself; he always had a driver – one of the ship's aircraft handlers, wearing his No. 1 uniform.

My team consisted of between 12 and 14 personnel; all of them aircraft engineers/mechanics, drafted to HMS *Hermes* as ship's company, to become part of the Aircraft Engineering Department (AED). We had now been a team for 16 months, so we all knew each other quite well; aware of our strengths and weaknesses. The officer in charge of the AED was a gentleman called Commander Stuart Barry, who came up through the ranks. He was known as the ship's Aircraft Engineering Officer (AEO).

I remember that, over the next few months, the senior officers (Captain, Commanders, etc.) would entertain local dignitaries onboard for lunch. Afterwards, Commander Barry would ask me what I had had for lunch. I would tell him, steak or lamb or salmon, etc. – even if it had been sausage and mash – and we would compare meals. What he failed to realise was that we had the chief caterer in our mess and he was responsible for all the victuals onboard! On one occasion, Commander Barry was left with cottage pie because they had run out of chicken (the guests had had the chicken). After that, on a few occasions I would get him a food parcel out of our mess, which he appreciated and thoroughly enjoyed!

CHAPTER THREE

News from Downing Street

~ • ~

When the news came from the Government that the Argentinians had invaded the Falkland Islands, the initial response was, "Why the f**k have they invaded a Scottish island?" I don't even think the navigating officer knew where the Falkland Islands were!

After learning that, where we were going and what the task ahead required the Royal Navy to carry out, all hell was let loose. Everyone onboard had the urgency to get the ship back to a seaworthy and fighting unit.

No doubt the squadrons, now at their parent air stations, had received the same news and were recalling all personnel who were on leave, to start the task of rebuilding their aircraft, making them serviceable ready to return to the ship. The ship was doing the same, along with all the other ships that were involved; everyone going about preparing their ship ready for war.

All of a sudden, over the weekend, people were returning from leave straight into preparing the ship for sea – no easy task for an aircraft carrier – knowing that the aircraft would be returning onboard while we were still alongside. The aircraft would usually return when we got to sea, sailing down the English Channel out of sight of land, somewhere off Portland Bill or Cornwall.

So, the scaffold that had gone up around the island had to be removed as soon as possible. Portacabins that housed the dockyard personnel's equipment had to be taken ashore from the flight deck and hangar, along with all their equipment. Decking that had been removed was now being replaced. Extra personnel were joining the ship (known in the Navy as 'a Pier Head Jump'). Everyone onboard was now working as a team – ship's crew, dockyard personnel – everyone feeling the pride of what they had been tasked to do, so that we could achieve something that hadn't been done for a long time: return a British land back to Britain; the United Kingdom.

The transport that had gone for servicing and repair to POST(N) had to be brought back to a serviceable condition and returned to the ship, including the Coles crane, before the aircraft could return onboard. We were all now working around the clock, and now we had the green overalls of the dockies, the sailors were wearing their blue overalls and every now and then you would see the white overalls of the officers getting involved and confusing the shit out of everyone. (They must be trained to do that, because it seems to come naturally to them!)

Now I had an extra responsibility of making sure that MacMo's ice cream parlour was stocked without an ounce of spare space in the freezer, so I grabbed one of the Land Rovers to take it for a test drive via the ice cream factory on the outskirts of Portsmouth. Mission accomplished, freezer now full, with help from my dedicated engineering team. I think they were hoping for a taster. No such luck!

The ship had a deadline for everything, which had to be met. All necessary tasks had to be completed in the correct sequence, so that the next step could be carried out, for example, scaffold removed so that the island could become operational again, flight deck cleared to accept the return of the ship's air group, flight deck painted with its mandatory markings, and so on.

What was going on below decks I hate to think: victuals being stowed; mess decks being made ready for extra personnel; hospital/sick bay being equipped for the unknown; engine room and boiler room checks being carried out along with the final servicing; galleys for extra personnel to feed; and the catering department making sure that the crew would have enough food to last until the first replenishment at sea (RAS) after leaving Pompey. Of course, all this activity was being mirrored on all the other ships being prepared for this journey into the unknown. The task that lay ahead; the questions being asked: How long? Where are we going? What will we be expected to do? Will we be working 24/7? What will it be like going to action stations for real? Will the young lads cope?

The average age of my team was between 22 and 24 – the same as the whole ship's company – so I felt responsible for them, to make sure we performed as a team to the best of our ability with the equipment we had, and, more importantly, that we **all** returned home safely, although nobody could tell what was hiding around the corner.

So that weekend was like any other day of the week but with a sense of urgency and all the time looking out for your shipmates and team.

The AED not only consisted of my department but also several workshops, which included electrical, avionics, tyres and wheels, the aircraft engine bay, the hydraulic bay, the mechanical workshop and the sheet metal workshop, so, with all these workshops, the manpower of the department was around 100 personnel and we were all doing our best to make sure that everything would be ready on time. Aircraft lifting equipment needed to be in date for test, test equipment needed to be calibrated and in date, which must be for the longest period possible plus a 10 per cent extension where possible because we were unaware of how long we were going to be away or whether we were even returning (which was on everyone's mind). Everyone onboard was also instructed to leave all valuables ashore, so we only took the necessaries with us.

CHAPTER FOUR

The Aircraft are Returning

~ • ~

As members of each department readied themselves and areas of the ship and flight deck so that the ship could accept the aircraft back onboard, the ship became a hive of activity.

The flight deck was ready, all the mandatory markings freshly painted, helicopter landing spots fresh and numbered, distance markings repainted (the wind over the deck and the weight of the Sea Harrier aircraft would determine the take-off run required by the Sea Harriers, which in the months to come would be critical), so all was ready to receive the first aircraft over the next few days prior to sailing. Even the flight deck tractors looked new, even though they were probably 25 years old; all nice yellow colours with large new numbers painted on them. Everybody was now feeling a sense of even more urgency and trepidation, hoping that we could all perform as expected, with no mishaps and, most of all, no accidents.

The news came that the aircraft would be on their way from their parent air stations, for example, Harriers from Yeovil. They would not be coming all at once but as they became serviceable. It was the same with the Sea King helicopters from their parent station at Culdrose in Cornwall.

Everyone on deck was ready (and because it was unusual to have the aircraft re-embark while still alongside, the locals were also in for a treat). Then there was the pipe (announcement over the ship's tannoy): "Hands to flying stations. Standby to recover. Sea Harriers."

So that everyone knew who everyone else was in reference to jobs and responsibilities, there was a colour system in place: each man wore a coloured surcoat (waistcoat). Yellow was for the aircraft handlers/ marshallers (easily recognisable by the pilots on landing, who would follow their instructions to clear the deck to make way for the next aircraft landing); white for the supervisor (officers, warrant officers, CPOs and petty officers), supervising the activities going on, on the deck, watching out for everyone, looking after their safety; blue for the aircraft handlers, who, once the aircraft was parked, would put the aircraft chocks in place;

brown for the aircraft mechanics (airframe and engines); green for the aircraft electricians; green with a black stripe for the radio mechanics; red for the aircraft armourers (who were going to be busy in the months to come); and white with a red cross for the first aiders (sick berth attendants). On the back of the surcoats there was a white square, which would have the wearer's name and the name of their squadron or department printed on it.

Then the pipe was made: "Aircraft estimated time of arrival. Standby to recover. Sea Harrier aircraft." Everyone was now in position: the marshallers, the fire suit men (to rescue the pilot if it didn't go to plan), my team and me standing by, hoping that we wouldn't be required.

After a while, all you can hear is the roar of the Pegasus engine as it flies over the dockyard and turns towards the ship, coming down the portside as it gets adjacent to the ship, and just above the level of the flight deck. The aircraft's nozzle points downwards to put the aircraft into the hover and the marshaller instructs the pilot to traverse to starboard over the flight deck until instructed to hover again by the marshaller over the flight deck before being instructed to land. Then it is moved out of the

Aircraft arriving, 1982. Flight deck busy.

Leaving Portsmouth for the South Atlantic (passing the Round Tower) April 1982.

way, so that the next one can land if required, but this time it goes silent as the Pegasus engine is shut down. The first one recovered safely without incident – which is not unusual because it has been done hundreds of times; the only difference being that it was done in the dockyard.

This was the procedure until all the aircraft due to join us in the dockyard were onboard. Once all the aircraft were onboard, witnessed by the locals and dockyard workers (who had all probably gone deaf although they would have enjoyed the free air show), the ground crews then joined the ship over the weekend, getting themselves settled in and everything stowed away.

In the meantime, while all this was going on, more and more lorries were arriving from all over the UK with urgent supplies and equipment, along with spare parts for the aircraft and parts for the aircraft on the small ships that had been turned around instead of coming home. In addition, there were parts and equipment coming onboard that were destined for Ascension Island, some 4,000 miles south in the Southern Atlantic.

The time was getting closer to our departure. Everything needed was nearly onboard: vegetables, toilet rolls, cleaning equipment, paint, brushes, scrubbers, etc. You name it, it was onboard, including pallets of ammunition. On one occasion, one of the forklifts was shifting a pallet of ammunition down the deck when smoke started exiting from under the engine cover, which the seat was attached to. The driver jumped off and the aircraft handlers (who are also the firemen) started getting the fire hoses out. I ran across and threatened them that if they covered the forklift in foam I'd have their guts for garters. I quickly removed the engine cover, threw it on the deck, saw the problem (diesel dripping on to the battery), knocked off the leads to the battery terminals and stopped the diesel leak. So, panic over. All sorted. Firemen pissed off because they weren't allowed to cover my lovely painted forklift in foam!

The day of departure. Everything and everyone coming onboard was onboard except for the Skipper's lovely blue Land Rover and two persons on the jetty: one of my lads, Alfie, and the Jossman. Alfie was there to hook the Land Rover on to our 14-ton Coles crane. Once this was done, the Jossman was there to make sure that Alfie came onboard with a kick up the arse!

All onboard. Nice Land Rover now in the hangar and stowed along with all the other Land Rovers and the ship's minibus (I forgot to mention that one). The Coles crane was finished with, so now it was lashed down for sea, like all the other equipment on the flight deck and in the hangar.

The aircraft onboard were now arranged on deck in Procedure Alpha positions (Procedure Alpha is the way in which the ship positions its crew around its decks when entering or leaving harbour), the crew were in their best uniforms to line the decks, the band was ready, the gangways had been removed, the berthing ropes let go, and the tugs took over, with our engines ready. Slowly, we slipped away from the quay and out to mid-stream. HMS *Invincible* was doing exactly the same at the same time.

Once in mid-channel, and with the assistance of the tugs, "Slow ahead, both", slowly we left Portsmouth dockyard into the Solent behind the *Invincible*. We, of course, were in our workshop in the forward hangar extension so couldn't be part of Procedure Alpha because we were in our working overalls. We were told afterwards that there were large crowds all along the seashore, and by the Round Tower, just outside the dockyard on the left. It was packed with well-wishers with Union Jacks flying, and home-made signs being held up with messages like 'Go get 'em, Jack'. It must have been an emotional sight, which I'm sure my young team were sorry to have missed, but we had a job to do. The date was 5 April 1982; the time 1045 exactly. Now onboard we had 12 Sea Harriers (more than we came in with), 17 Sea King helicopters on deck, Royal Marine Commandos, some RAF chappies (not sure why!) and of course extra crew to carry out extra tasks. We were still to bring onboard the Admiral and his staff.

Now at sea, into the unknown towards what lay ahead…

"Training, training, training"

"Exercise, exercise, exercise"

"Fire, fire, fire!"

"Action stations, action stations, action stations!"

"Crash on deck, crash on deck, crash on deck!"

"Damage control, damage control, damage control!"

"Action messing, action messing, action messing!"

…and anything else that might happen.

All targets were reached to have the ship ready on time.

Now we were making our way into the Solent, past the forts at No Man's Land and Spit Bank. Built to protect the dockyard and surrounding areas but never used in anger, they were at the time of war manned by the Army; each with more than 1,000 personnel on them. No Man's Land had only six sinks, that were for officers use only. The lower ranks had to go for a dip in the sea if they wanted to wash! Maybe that's where they got their nickname 'Pongoes'. Where the army goes, the pong goes!

Nearly everyone onboard now settled down to a routine – which is normal once a ship gets to sea – all doing what they were responsible for. No passengers. Everyone had a job to do, from the Captain down to the sailors keeping the ship clean.

As people walked around the ship, they would come across old pals and mates from serving on previous ships and squadrons, especially from the squadrons from the air arm of the navy; the Fleet Air Arm (FAA). We were a small unit compared to the Royal Navy, so it wasn't long before you bumped into people you knew from previous squadrons or Royal Naval Air Stations (RNASs). I came across quite a few old mates. After all, I had been in the Navy for 21 years by this time.

Onboard we now had 845 Commando Squadron of the Royal Marines with their Sea King Mk4 aircraft painted in dark green. Their aircraft was also maintained by FAA engineers because the Royal Marines are part of the Royal Navy. I bumped into an old pal, Willie Monahan, so we had lots to talk about.

We were now on passage, down the English Channel. Lots of good luck messages had been received onboard. Everyone was making sure that all their equipment was stowed and lashed securely, in the event of hitting some rough weather around the Bay of Biscay as we headed south.

During the day, there were the comings and goings of helicopters bringing on more stores, equipment and personnel who couldn't make it to join the ship before we left. Also, to deliver personnel and mail ashore.

In my section, I put my team into watches, where I would take the day shift (0800–2000) and my PO electrician, Nigel Gentry, would cover the night shift (2000–0800). We each had a team of lads, although I had a larger team due to the fact that I thought we would be busier during the day, and the night shift would have more of the routine checks to do.

As always, on a daily basis at sea, I would pay a visit to the ship's Aircraft Maintenance Control Office (AMCO) to have a look at the signals that the ship had received to see if there were any that affected our department. This is where I would usually meet up with Commander Barry along with my immediate boss, Lt Trevor Whiting, and other senior rates of the AED.

At lunchtime, it became apparent that from now on the ship was on rations, so food was limited. Although there were tons of food onboard and stored in passageways, we didn't know how long it was going to have to last before the first RAS, where we would meet up with our Royal Fleet Auxiliary (RFA) ship to get fresh supplies. Also, some of the victuals we were carrying were destined for some of the ships that were not coming home but were being rerouted south. When in range of these ships, the helicopters could deliver the supplies, stores and spare parts via underslung loads.

The first day nearly over, what would tomorrow bring? My last task of the day would be to phone the bridge to ask the officer of the watch if he could make a pipe to announce: "The ice cream parlour is now open and will remain open until 2100." The ice cream parlour was a chest freezer which I kept in my MT spare parts store. My first customer on previous trips had always been Lt Schoolie, and, yes, true to form, he was the first one that night, in his black trousers, immaculate, crisp, white, short-sleeved shirt with lieutenant's epaulettes on the shoulders and a black cummerbund.

"The usual, sir?"

"Yes please. One scoop of vanilla."

"That's 50p. Prices still the same although I might have to increase them or use a smaller scoop if the demand increases with all those trained Royal Marine Commando killers onboard!"

The next day: Tuesday.

What a way to be woken up. "Exercise, exercise, exercise!" and "Hands to action stations, hands to action stations, hands to action stations!" We were all in our bunks, not expecting that one. I think that there were more people injured that morning as we all (six of us) leapt out of bed and landed on the deck at the same time, legs and arms everywhere, trying to put on each other's overalls and steaming boots. After all, they were the same colour!

So off we went to action stations: the two engine room boys off to the engine room and, with the latches closed, more or less locked in apart from a small kidney hatch within the main hatch; the two squadron engineers off to the hangar or flight deck; one AED engineer to the hangar extension to his workshop; and me up to the flight deck. At first, as I was making my way up to the deck, I would give others coming down priority. That soon changed with the emergency that was to come, when I would shout, "Get out my f****** way!"

This was the first action stations exercise. Once everyone was closed up, we had a report back from the Skipper on the bridge – or it might have been the Commander – to say that he wasn't happy because it had taken too long (I think about 20 minutes or slightly longer. We practised this every day until we arrived at the Total Exclusion Zone (TEZ): an area of 200 miles around the Falkland Islands. The first time we went to action stations for real it was at Ascension Island, when someone spotted a submarine periscope (I believe it was Russian). By this time, we had got going to action stations down to between five and seven minutes, which was a great achievement for a ship this size.

The rest of the Tuesday was spent preparing your departments for the unknown: carrying out exercise after exercise; checking the firefighting equipment, first aid boxes and breathing apparatus; charging bottles; making sure that damage control equipment was serviceable; and checking the splinter boxes used to temporarily repair holes in the ship's side below the waterline.

Of course, while all this is going on we were at 'flying stations': the Sea Kings flying underslung loads here, there and everywhere, bringing more people onboard, taking people to other ships. The Harrier crews were familiarising themselves with taking off and landing on the busy deck. Being on deck you had to have your wits about you. It was so noisy, you could only rely on your eyes and team to watch out for each other.

Being in charge of my team, and a senior rate, I had a radio, which meant that I was in constant communication with Flyco, so I could keep my guys informed about what was going on.

There were several exercises carried out throughout the ship and on the deck: exercise 'Fire Fire Fire Boiler Room' and exercise 'Crash on Deck. Salvage Team Close Up', for example.

Also, the Royal Marines had to exercise, keeping them fit, so the flight deck was made available for them to train for an hour. This was to become a daily event for them. On top of that, they carried out some tasks throughout the ship.

The ship was now full of equipment, machinery and ammunitions, and it became even more difficult to move about. It was difficult enough during normal operations but this was extra hard. When we exercised action stations, you had to wear your anti-flash gear, which consisted of a hood made of cotton, with only your eyes visible, and gauntlets to cover your hands and arms. This was to protect you from, say, a fireball, if we were hit. Also, we had to carry our gas masks, our once only survival suit, which was bright orange, and our life jackets. On top of that, I also had my radio attached to my belt along with my knife, which would be handy for emergencies and might be required to release something in a hurry, for example, if I was going into the water, I wouldn't need my steaming boots, so I could cut the laces and get rid of them before jumping in.

So now the scene was set. The following days were much the same: everyone going about their tasks as normal but with all sorts of exercises going on. Everything started to become routine apart from the odd visitor to the ship, meals being rationed, and coping with the weather. Our first stop was going to be Ascension Island in about 14 days' time.

What we did notice as we progressed south was the weather getting hotter, so when exercising with your anti-flash gear on it was becoming unbearably hot but it had to be done – even the Skipper was wearing his. We knew we were going south because the sun was on the port side in the morning and went down on the starboard side.

As the days passed, and more and more exercises were carried out, precious seconds were taken off the times. This could save the ship if it was hit. All of this was controlled by the Damage Control HQ (known as HQ1). The Seamen Department were going through their damage control routines, knowing exactly what to do and where the necessary equipment was. After all, they might be required to save the ship from fire, flooding, etc. Everything had to be second nature to everyone.

The news we were receiving wasn't good…it was becoming more and more apparent that the unknown was now becoming known and that we were going to war!

The atmosphere throughout the ship changed. All mirrors, glass, etc. throughout the ship had sticky tape over them to prevent them from splintering if hit. All valuables had already been left ashore. I believe that the officers' piano was also left behind. What a shame!

Lots of good wishes and good luck messages were still being received. The ship's complement was told to instruct their crews to make out wills. Everyone was issued with fireproof dog tags, on which you had to stamp your name, rank, official number and religion. Everyone was concerned now and put even more urgency into everything they did. Before we reached the South, personnel with accommodation (mess deck, as it is known in the Royal Navy) below the waterline had to move above it, in case of a torpedo hit, so this meant that above the waterline it was more crowded, with people sleeping in the passageways. Some went to sleep with their anti-flash gear on. I remember seeing one guy who had his hood on and he had written on it in black marker pen, 'Hello Mum'. He must have been about 19 years old. Sailors never lose their sense of humour.

We were now getting further south and closer to the Equator and our first stop: Ascension Island. The temperature was getting extremely hot, compared with the UK, rising daily.

Ice cream stock was also now getting extremely low; the Schoolie having increased his daily dose. The Royal Marines preferred the strawberry flavour. I don't know if it was the taste or the nice pink colour! With stocks getting low, I had to take some drastic action, which I did. I went to the Operations Officer and explained the situation. He said: "Bloody hell, Chief! We can't have that! There will be a mutiny onboard. There is a Sea King going ashore to Ascension with CPO Kilkullen. You jump onboard and see if you can get some from the Yanks. The chopper is leaving at 0700. See what you can do."

That was a turn-up for the books! Next morning, up bright and early, into our flying overalls, life jackets and flying helmets, airborne dead on

Relaxing day at sea on the way south, 1982.

0700 (good job it was Navy pilots. If it had been the RAF, they would have still been in bed, waiting on a cup of tea!). So off we went to this rock sticking out of the Atlantic.

We landed at the airport, which is called Wideawake, due to the fact that there is a particular type of bird that lives there – nowhere else in the world – that chirps constantly through the night on the windowsills, keeping you awake. Hence, the name of the airport being 'Wideawake'. On arrival, we couldn't believe our eyes. There were aircraft everywhere: Hercules C130s of the RAF, and Belfast aircraft, which were ex-RAF. Now belonging to 'Heavy Lift', they were unloading their cargos: Wessex helicopters; Lynx helicopters; rockets; ammunition; stores of all kinds. You name it, and it was coming down the ramp of these large cargo aircraft.

In one area, the helicopters that had arrived in the back of aircraft were being reassembled by the FAA aircraft engineers. They had probably been working through the night to get them ready to fly as soon as possible.

As you made your way around the island, you would come across people you knew from previous drafts you had had; just like onboard. There were soldiers, sailors and Royal Marine Commandos everywhere. The ships' helicopters were in abundance, ferrying people and stores out to their mother ships.

The crew making the most of it before we reach the 'TEZ'.

I nearly forgot the reason why I was ashore: to purchase ice cream. So, off we went searching for who would have access to the ice cream; my pocket with a few bob in it. We went to the main galley; everyone there was eating breakfast. I was pointed in the direction of the main man and tried to make a deal with him. He had 300 litres of ice cream, but the miserable Yank wouldn't even let me have one scoop. I was pissed off about that! I started to think about the impending mutiny and that the cost of flying me ashore for ice cream must have run into a few hundred pounds, so, in true naval tradition that Lord Nelson himself would have been proud of, no, we didn't pillage the ice cream; we found the bar and nearly got pissed to drown our sorrows. Well, we had a pocketful of money that was burning a hole in it, and our flight back wasn't until 1800. What else could we do?

So, now back onboard, empty-handed, what could I do to make the ice cream last? Perhaps I could swap the ice cream scoop for a teaspoon? I thought, I don't think the Royal Marines will notice, but I knew the Schoolie would.

Back to the serious business now. Before we arrived at Ascension Island, we had one rest day. It might have been to celebrate the crossing of the Equator, when King Neptune and his men come onboard, and the Captain asks permission to cross the Equator. It's a bit of fun, where a selected few – usually the officers – are covered in a horrible green goo, are then sat down one by one in a chair, which is tilted backwards and are then dropped into a makeshift pool/tank made out of canvas. If you're first in, it's not too bad, but, as the day goes on, the water is horrible with thick, slimy stuff.

While this is going on, the majority of the crew that are not on watch and can be spared (the ship still has to operate) make use of the deck for some recreation: sunbathing. For those who had spent the last 10 to 12 days below deck, it was very noticeable. They were really 'paley waley'. Some even looked as though they had on a set of long johns!

There was a beard-growing contest going on while we made our passage south, but now was 'Judgement Day' and time to shave them off, so that if, later on, if required to don your gas mask (gas respirator), it would fit properly with an airtight seal. So, now that you had people who had removed their sets (that's what beards are called in the Navy), their faces were two-tone: red and white around the chin and cheeks, like a Neapolitan ice cream, dark on the top (hair); red in the middle and white on the bottom!

Another funny thing that happened was that one of the Regulating Petty Officers (RPOs) who belonged to the Master at Arms team, came on to the flight deck dressed as an Argentinian, with a sombrero on his head and a strip of ammunition slung across his chest. One of the members of the Press onboard (I think it was Brian Hanrahan) interviewed him and asked him, "What will you and your men do when the British arrive?" He replied, "Wen de Brutush arrive me an ma man's will fuks orf out of it. We no lik a fightin."

The day over and back to the serious business of getting the ship even more prepared for what lay ahead and over the horizon.

CHAPTER FIVE

Arrival at Ascension Island

~ • ~

We arrived at Ascension Island, and anchored off shore because there was only a small harbour, which serviced the whole island.

No Sea Harriers flying today, since we were at anchor and there was no wind over the deck, but the helicopters of 826 and 845 Squadrons were extremely busy flying back and forth from the island, shifting loads from the *Hermes* to ashore ready to be transferred to other ships.

HMS *Invincible* had not yet arrived. Apparently, she had to reduce speed, because she was one of the navy's new ships, she would vibrate excessively, so had to reduce speed to reach an acceptable level of vibration. It must have been very uncomfortable for those onboard; not to mention the embarrassment and the mickey-taking that was going to be issuing in their direction.

While there, my boss 'Whato', came up to me and informed me that HMS *Yarmouth* (a frigate with a Wasp helicopter onboard) was having problems with their HIFR and could I go to the radio room, down in the ship's bilges, where they would get in touch with the *Yarmouth* so that I could speak to the flight's Senior Maintenance Rating (SMR). He added that I wasn't to mention any names, because "You don't know who might be listening." So, our radio operator got in contact with the *Yarmouth* and put me on the radio. I said, "I believe you have a problem with your HIFR?" The answer I got back wasn't what I expected. "Is that you, George?" I replied, "Is that you, Dave?" Whato behind me was shouting, "No names!" I nearly pissed myself laughing. Between Dave and me, we sorted out the problem.

Dave used to be my next-door neighbour when I lived on Portland and was serving at HMS *Osprey*. We were old pals from way back. Not knowing it at this time, but I was to meet up with him again 'down south'.

The *Invincible* eventually arrived and anchored close by to us, where you could see their helicopters carrying out similar tasks to ours.

I met up with another old pal. He had come down to Ascension Island with us and was in 845 Squadron. We met in the hangar, just beside the

Anchored off the Ascension Island.

hangar extension, and he asked me what was going on. I replied, "I don't know. Why?" He replied, "The squadron is being disembarked here and going on to either HMS *Fearless* or *Intrepid*, with the Booties (Royal Marine Commandoes). I knew that if they were going on to one of the assault ships they would be going ashore on to the Falkland Islands somewhere, as one, if not the first, of the advanced groups, and that would include the FAA aircraft engineers, to maintain their aircraft in the field. I was hoping that I was wrong. I said, "Take care and make sure you keep your head down. See you sometime." We gave each other a hug and off he went. I haven't seen him since. I do know that he was okay, but, if and when I do see him again, I'm going to have it out with him. I found out after he had left the ship that he had been using my mess number to buy his drinks! Not just the gins but the bloody tonics as well! My bill was over £40. With the price of drinks being low, he must have had gallons! Nonetheless, if I do meet up with him again, I know it will be a good night, drinking and talking about the old times.

I can't remember how long we were at anchor for, but I do know that we made a hasty departure. It was reported that a submarine's periscope had been sighted. You can't tell what nationality a submarine is just by its periscope. Seeing one or detecting a submarine that you don't know is a captain's worst nightmare. So, it was "Hands to Action Stations". Royal Naval captains are aware of what the consequences could be if the sighting is ignored. During the 1940s, during World War II, Scapa Flow in the Orkneys, a natural inland anchorage, was judged by the Royal Navy as being a safe anchorage for their North Atlantic fleet. Ships of all descriptions (battleships, destroyers, frigates, mine sweepers, trawlers, supply ships, etc.) would return, to be rearmed with munitions, victuals, changes of personnel and, of course, fuel (either coal or oil). One night, under the cover of darkness, the German U-boat, *U47*, captained by Captain Prinz, managed to navigate through the barriers and submarine nets and entered Scapa Flow. They managed to take bearings and aim on to one of the Royal Navy's capital ships: HMS *Royal Oak*. They fired three torpedoes. I believe one hit the bow section; another midships, shortly afterwards. Some of the ship's crew thought that it was their own shells exploding due to them having self-ignited, which was a known possibility, before realising what was going on. The *U47* had made a hasty escape and was now back in the Solway Firth, with a submerged course, set for Germany. On their return to Germany, Captain Prinz and his crew received a hero's welcome, and he was decorated with Germany's highest military award.

Back in Scapa Flow, where the *Royal Oak* was well ablaze, rescue boats were doing their best to pick up survivors. A total 800 members of the crew were lost; the bodies recovered were buried in the Naval Cemetery on the Isle of Hoy. The *Royal Oak* is still lying on the seabed in Scapa Flow and is a war grave, which is out of bounds to divers, except for one day of the year, when Royal Naval divers go down and replace the White Ensign of the Royal Navy. So, you can understand why, if the Captain sees an unknown periscope, his bum will start twitching, along with everyone else's onboard!

Now we were underway again, along with the other ships that had gathered at Ascension Island.

We were closed up at action stations, continuing our journey south, with haste, to clear the area as quickly as possible. Once clear, we were stood down. Everyone could now take off their anti-flash gear and stow it away in their gas mask bag, always ready to put it back on again at a second's notice. You became accustomed to the procedure. As soon as you heard the first note of the klaxon, you automatically reached inside your respirator bag, took out your anti-flash gear and put it on.

What I did notice was the way in which the ships were communicating with each other. It was not by radio, but by 'signal lamp' or 'Aldus lamp', sending messages and signals in Morse Code between ships. The speed at which the flag wavers (Signals Branch) could send signals and also write down the replies was very impressive. There were always two wavers: one to read the incoming message and the other to write it down.

Also, while at Ascension Island, I noticed the number of ships there; they seemed to be increasing by the hour. Not only Royal Navy ships, but also Merchant Navy ships, stretching back to the horizon. They had been taking up from trade (STUFT, as they were known). It was quite a sight and comforting to know that you weren't on your own. Even the Royal Navy's survey ships were there, being used as hospital ships, with big red crosses painted on their sides, including HMS *Herald* (which I served on in 1976/77), HMS *Hecla* and HMS *Hydra*.

Going further south, the weather was getting warmer. Now getting into a state of complete readiness, aircraft now doing some serious flying, the flight deck was buzzing with what was going on and what was expected of us: the Sea King helicopters, hovering, with their Asdic radar in the water, pinging for any unwanted submarines in the area around the fleet; the Sea Harriers, practising firing or dropping all types of weapons (rockets, cluster bombs, 1,000-lb bombs, etc.). We had to get it right; we couldn't afford any mistakes. No room for errors. After all, the Argentinians had nearly 300 aircraft. We had 21 or 24, before losses, which we couldn't really afford.

Then, there was the ship, which had to be prepared from attack; whether it be from the air or from submarines. The ship no longer had anti-aircraft guns (Boofers) or Sea Cat missiles; they had been removed because they were obsolete. The ship's defence was now its aircraft. The added defence onboard were crew members stationed around the ship and on and around the ship's island with machine guns. Remember, the most dangerous thing on earth is a sailor with a gun! I pitied the Argies if they ever came across one!

Part of getting the ship ready meant that the ship's mast and aerials above the island had to be painted grey; the same colour as the rest of the ship. The reason for this was that, if the ship had a distinctive colour change, grey to black, a submarine apparently could work out how far the ship was from the submarine, which meant that they would know what range we were before firing their torpedoes. I remember going on deck the day they were painting the aerials and mast. I looked up and saw these sailors sitting in bosuns' chairs. painting away quite merrily, using long-handled paintbrushes, painting out the black and replacing it with ship's grey. Unfortunately, parked below where they were painting were the Sea Harriers of 800 Squadron. Well, along came one of 800 Squadron's

AEOs. When he saw his lovely fighting machines, he went ballistic. His aircraft were now speckled in the ship's dark sea grey! He wasn't a happy chappie, although everyone else who had seen it did have a bit of a laugh about it. Sailors have a great sense of humour; especially at someone else's expense and when someone is going to be dropped in the shit for it.

By now we were even closer to our action area. New faces seemed to appear from nowhere. Now we had the SAS and SBS onboard. Where they came from nobody knew. They arrived with all their equipment, even fold-up canoes, which I think they kept in their back pockets! They never wore any rank on their uniforms, which was an advantage to them because it meant that they could go and eat in the junior rates galley then come up to the senior rates galley for a second meal. I think they deserved it. After all, where they were going I think the food was going to be limited or non-existent. Anyway, I wasn't going to be the one to stop them, telling them that they couldn't do that.

I was speaking to one of them; a staff sergeant I think. They had been in Kenya training when they got the word. They were going to the Falklands, the guy I was speaking to told me. He had been to Kenya with his squadron as a last trip because he was due to retire from the Services when he returned to the UK. Unfortunately, his retirement was postponed until after the Falklands.

Also now onboard was Admiral Sandy Woodward (a submariner) and his staff, who thought that they were better than anyone else. I recall that, one morning during the conflict, I was just finishing my breakfast and three CPOs from the Admiral's staff came in. They all went for their breakfasts. One of the CPOs took three rolls (one each). Once they had eaten them, another CPO got up and took another three (one each). So, I starting watching them and, when they had eaten the second batch, the third CPO went for another three. I got up and said, "What do you think you're doing? It's one roll each. There are people still on watch that have not had their breakfasts." The CPOs took the rolls and threw them back in the tray, saying that they didn't want them anyway. I don't know who these people think they are. Just because they are the Admiral's goffers they think that they can do what they please. Also, they were guests on my ship and were strutting around as if they owned it.

Everyone onboard was now getting used to the food rationing: the same veg (broccoli and broad beans); one bread roll at breakfast, at 4 o'clock (4 o'clockers); and cake on Tuesdays and Thursdays instead of every day. We had run out of salad. There were no chips; only powdered mashed potatoes. Also powdered milk, which is a grey colour when mixed, and powdered eggs for scrambling, which were a yellowish grey colour.

People were starting to lose weight, which I'm sure wasn't just down to the rationing but because of the heat and keeping up with the exercises, usually held at lunchtime outside my workshop (so I didn't have far to go). We would also go to fitness training in the late afternoon on the flight deck if it was available and they had finished flying. If they hadn't, it was back into the hangar and we would carry on there.

As for the ice cream parlour, stock was now drastically low, so it was now time to get in contact with other ships to see if they had any to spare. This wasn't successful either, so I started opening for fewer hours when routine permitted.

CHAPTER SIX

25 April 1982

~ • ~

On 25 April, with five days still to go before we reached the TEZ, we got news that South Georgia had been recaptured. A cheer went up throughout the whole ship. We had started to make progress and the Argentinians now knew that we meant business. The feeling on the ship was one of jubilation.

The Argentinian submarine, the *Santé Fe*, had been disabled, having been hit on the conning tower by a missile and holed. We had lost two Wessex helicopters due to snow white-out. The third helicopter, another Wessex, had managed to recover the crews and passengers (Royal Marines) and got them back to their ship safely. The Arctic training, for

Rough weather in the South Atlantic.

both the Royal Marines and the FAA pilots, came to good use here.

However, not all went smoothly. Before we reached the TEZ, the *Hermes* was transferring either Royal Marines, SAS or SBS to HMS *Fearless* or *Intrepid*, one of our assault ships, when one of 845 Squadron's Sea King helicopters crashed as it neared the ship. They say that it sustained a bird strike and crashed into the sea, which by now, because the temperature had plummeted, was freezing cold. The aircraft turned upside down and, with it being night-time (approximately 2300), it was difficult to escape the aircraft. I believe that all souls were lost. This was our first tragic incident. The mood onboard the *Hermes*, and no doubt the other ships in the fleet, went the other way: from taking back South Georgia, to sadness, asking ourselves, What next? What's around the corner? What's over the horizon? No one knew.

We had now reached the last few days before we would be in our operating area. The weather had definitely got worse, with rough seas, much colder temperatures to what we had been experiencing and heavy rain.

The ship was now ready as much as it could be for the forthcoming action. My lads had prepared themselves well: working as a team; being in the right place at the right time (and also at a moment's notice); knowing

Above: Rough weather. Inset: Bit of roughers.

RAS. Taking on fuel in South Atlantic.

what each other was capable of; looking out for each other; and knowing where each other was at any time of the day or night.

The journey south had been hard work; more or less dealing with every possible situation that could happen to us: fire; air attacks; submarine attacks; man overboard; loss of steering; action messing; crash on deck; fire on deck; and action stations (now down to six or seven minutes, but we were still trying to reduce this even more).

The Sea Kings were still doing their pinging tasks. The aircraft were also armed with torpedoes, ready in case any Argentinian submarines were detected. The Sea Harriers had also completed their practices: rocket firings; bomb dropping (of several types); and firing their cannons. Night-flying tasks and deck landings day and night were also complete. Everything from now on (two days away) was going to be for real.

The armourers had also been practising the roll changes of the aircraft, changing from rockets to bombs and vice versa, as quickly as possible. The flight deck had two 'bomb dumps', as they are called. These were areas on the flight deck – one just forward of the island; the other to the aft of the island – where munitions (bombs, rockets, depth charges, etc.) were stowed ready for use at a moment's notice. As they were used, replacements were brought up from below.

There was now much activity on deck.

On the way south, the ship had carried out several RASs, replacing the ship's fuel, aircraft fuel, victuals, beer and even toilet rolls; more or less everything that had been used had to be replaced. The RAS was carried out about every 7 to 10 days; it might have been less. But no ice cream.

When we had a chance just to look out to the open sea, we could see the other ships in our group, and aircraft flying around, taking off and landing back on. Where they had been, what they were doing, only they knew.

We saw a lot of sea life on the way down south: dolphins swimming alongside the ship, leaping out of the water and over the ship's bow wave; porpoises; whales in the distance blowing air from their blowholes; sharks looking for an easy meal; and flying fish skimming over the water, just above the surface. Watching these fish for a moment took your mind off the task ahead and gave you something to write home about, which would hopefully also take your loved ones' minds off what we were doing.

So now our final RAS had been completed. The ship was really low in the water (no distinct line was visible between the water and the waterline, now all grey; the black having been painted out). Everything was full: fuel, aircraft fuel, ammunitions, stores, including victuals, etc. Our next RAS would be after we had been in action and depending on what the ship had been doing.

CHAPTER SEVEN

30 April / 1 May 1982

~ • ~

The date was now 30 April. The Argentinians knew we were coming. They must have. All they had to do was watch the BBC World News. Members of the Press onboard our ships were relaying back to the UK what we were up to and more or less our position, and were getting paid plenty for it compared to the men in the Forces. I sometimes wondered whose side they were on.

During the night, Captain Middleton came on the ship's broadcast and praised us all for our professionalism in the way in which we had prepared the ship for the unknown. He said, "Tomorrow is the big day. Good luck, and thank you all for your help in making the *Hermes* the best worked-up ship in the Task Force." (Actually, I don't think he said that, but I thought I'd put it in to upset the *Invincible*. A bit of internal rivalry! However, we were all there as one and for one objective: to free the Falkland Islands from the Argentinians. To free them from the sea.)

The next day, 1 May, up as usual, showered, bunk made and stowed, everything stowed away and secured. After breakfast – and one roll – back to the cabin, on with overalls, on with white surcoat, on with belt with knife and radio, on with respirator bag (with anti-flash hood and gloves inside), and on with pouch with once-only survival suit (I hope I don't have to use this; the water is bloody freezing). I then take my flight deck helmet in my hand, take a last look around the cabin, making sure everything is stowed away. I close the door and make my way down to the workshop, where my team is, including the night shift, who are going off watch and will be back at 2000 to take over unless there is action stations, when they will man the workshop while the day shift is closed up on the flight deck.

The time now is around 0800. The Captain once again addresses the ship's company: "Earlier this morning, an RAF Vulcan aircraft had flown down from Ascension Island and bombed the airport at Stanley, after carrying out several inflight refuelling tasks on the way. So now it is our turn."

The call goes out: "Hands to Flying Stations", so the team and I make our way up to the flight deck, while the nightwatch goes and gets some well-earned rest.

Once on deck, we have our daily checks to do: inspections on the aircraft refuelling hoses and points; crane operating correctly; always standing by to rectify any defect or problems on any of the flight deck vehicles, tractors, forklifts, etc. Then checking the equipment in the aircraft salvage locker, making sure it is in the correct place and is still serviceable and intact, which it should be because it hasn't been touched since yesterday.

When the checks are completed, we remain on deck during flying stations, the team positioning themselves in or near the aircraft salvage locker; a small room in the island outboard of the flight deck. I will be in the ACR, where the aircrew come in and sign for their aircraft. I am positioned there so that if anything goes wrong I will be one of the first to know, after the Aircraft Control Room Officer (ACRO), Lt Jim Broadley.

As soon as the RAF Vulcan bomber had bombed Stanley and woke the Argentinians up, our Harriers, already manned and armed with 1,000-lb bombs and with engines running ready, go and do their stuff on the Argentinians, before they go back to sleep, which I very much doubt was on their minds, not knowing what hit them.

My first task on this day, which was to become a memorable one during the first launch of the day, is to keep personnel, especially reporters, from crossing the safety line. They seem to think that they can do whatever they want and go wherever they please. The safety line is a narrow painted line, which runs the length of the flight deck and denotes the edge of the runway, where the aircraft operate from, so my job is to make sure that personnel don't cross it.

The Press were by now becoming a nuisance, getting in the way of everyone. If they could, they would have sat on the pilot's laps!

The first aircraft get a green light from Flyco, the Flight Deck Officer (FDO) raises his green flag and waves it above his head. The pilot gives him the thumbs-up; he's ready to go. The FDO checks that everything is clear, waits for the ship's bow to start rising with the swell and drops his green flag. Engine already at full power, brakes released, and off the pilot goes up the ramp and is airborne. The aircraft drops out of sight. I hear in my headset that, with the aircraft fully laden with two 1,000-lb bombs and full fuel, the pilot should have been further down the deck, giving him a longer take-off run. Fortunately, he managed to stay airborne. If he hadn't, that would have been a great loss to the ship. The next aircraft is quickly marshalled out of the way and positioned on to the side lift and parked up, so that the other aircraft can get off with the correct take-off run and avoid an incident. The pilot of the second aircraft, which is now parked up on the side lift with engines running, waiting on all the other aircraft to take off, is not happy. With a clenched fist, he is striking the inside of the cockpit to release his frustration and is probably in radio contact with Flyco, letting them know that he isn't a happy bunny. I wish I could have listened in on that one-way conversation!

Once all the other aircraft have taken off, the pilot is then marshalled back down the deck to the correct position and the green flag is raised. Thumbs-up from the pilot, bows rising, green flag down, brakes released, aircraft rolling down the deck gathering speed instantly, up the ramp and airborne, now on his way with the other aircraft to various targets on the Falkland Islands, to drop their bombs on the unsuspecting Argentinians.

The flight deck is now clear of all aircraft, flight deck crews wondering what's going on, talking among themselves, pleased that the launch of the aircraft has gone well, without incident or problem (apart from the one). The Press are still getting in the way, trying to take pictures of anything and everything.

I'm with my team, thanking them for a great effort, when, all of a sudden, over the flight deck tannoy comes the announcement: "Stand to, stand to, stand to!" All flight deck personnel take cover at the rush, in the catwalks (area that you can drop into, which runs around the edge of the flight deck and houses the aircraft refuelling points, electrical points and fire points). "Exocet missile launched at 45 miles." I am asked by one of my lads, "What the f**k's going on?" I say, "Follow me." As we are running down the deck, they fire chaff (strips of tinfoil) from the island above us; something they haven't done before. How it works is that they fire the chaff so that it goes above the ship, making the ship look bigger than it is to the Exocet. The missile will then rise up to the bigger target and fly over the ship. Well, that's the theory. Somehow it doesn't make us feel any safer.

When we get aft of the island, we jump into the catwalk. There are four or five of us. We are not happy. This can't be happening to us; we are the Royal Navy. Then one of the team says, "George, look!" I say, "Keep your f*****g head down!" and he says again, "F*****g look, Chief!" So I do. When I look out at where we are in the catwalk, I look on the flight deck next to us, about four feet away, and see the rear ammunitions dump. I say, "Oh, shit! Let's get the f**k out of here! Follow me!" So we all get back on to the flight deck and run like hell over to the other side. While we are running for our lives, I hear in my headset, "Chief McDonald, take cover!", so I give the thumbs-up to Flyco and we all jump into the catwalk on the port side and take cover.

It's a strange feeling, being in a position where you're not in control and not knowing what or if something is going to happen. It was certainly a relief to know that the danger was over, just as quickly as it occurred. What happened to the missile we would never know. It probably burnt itself out because it launched from too far away, so we hoped that any future attacks with this type of missile would be carried out from the same distance or even further away.

It doesn't take long before we are back on deck, chatting about what has just happened and pleased that it didn't develop into something more serious. Then comes the announcement over the flight deck tannoy: "Standby to recover the Harriers", so my team and I go to our positions: me to the ACR; my team to the salvage locker at the back of the island. Of course, on our minds is, I hope we are not required.

The aircraft all return safely, all serviceable apart from one, which has a hole in its vertical fin the size of a golf ball.

All serviceable aircraft are now being rearmed, either with bombs, or role changed for rockets. Once they are all fuelled up, turnaround inspections are carried out by the Squadron engineers and the pilots changed over. They're ready for the off once again.

This time, the 'media' knows where they can go and the areas where they can't. Mind you, a lot of the people on deck would like to tell them where to go permanently!

The aircraft have clearance to start their engines. Once started, the engineers remove the last two nose undercarriage lashings, give the pilots the thumbs-up, meaning that the aircraft is all his, and good luck, see you when you return. The aircraft is then handed over to the aircraft marshaller in his yellow surcoat, who is now standing in front of the aircraft, with his right arm bent at the elbow, at a right angle in front of him with his fist clenched, meaning 'brakes on'. When the marshaller gets the all-clear from Flyco and the deck area is clear of engineers, etc., and it's his aircraft's turn to be launched, he opens his clenched fist to signal to the pilot 'brakes off', then he puts his arms out to the side, bent at the elbows, and moves them from side to side, as if he is using them to wave to the pilot. This instructs the pilot that it's now time to taxi the aircraft forward. After a while, he signals to the pilot that he needs to take instructions from the next marshaller, who positions the aircraft on the correct spot for 'take off', then passes him over to the FDO, who launches the aircraft after instructions from Flyco. Then it's thumbs-up from the pilot, brakes on, throttles open, max power, green flag raised, wait for the bow to start rising, green flag down, brakes off, and off the aircraft goes, trundling down the deck. All you hear is the roar of the engine, a cracking sound, and the aircraft reaches the bottom of the ramp, shoots up the ramp to reach take-off speed and is airborne on its way for its second mission of the day, along with all the other aircraft, which have gone through the same procedure before take-off. The flight deck crews are now getting all their equipment ready for their aircraft's return, which they know would be in about 40 minutes' time.

Now that the deck is clear, it is the helicopters' turn to return onboard for refuelling, or for crew changes or pick-up loads to transfer to other ships. Everyone is busy, busy; my team checking that the flight deck vehicles are performing properly, carrying out any repairs that can be done quickly to keep them serviceable.

The aircraft that was damaged on the last sortie is now down in the hangar getting 'battle damaged repair' to its vertical fin by the Squadron engineers. It should be serviceable for the next sortie. When repairs are being carried out under these circumstances, a lot of common sense and experience comes into it. The engineers know exactly what they're capable of, get the correct metal, cut it to the correct size, clean out the damaged area, pick up the frames and 'stringers' (part of the fin structure) and, using oversized rivets, stick the patch on, give it a coat of paint and send it back on deck. Job done That will do till we get home (TWDTWGH). This is common practice in the FAA. It's not like being on land, where you can go to the shops to get what is required. We have to make do with what we have on the ship and **make** it work, and this is what the FAA does best. An aircraft is meant to fly. The FAA will get it flying.

The aircraft are now returning from their second sortie. The media are all over the aircraft and crews like a rash, trying to get a story. All the aircraft are back safely and no damage this time. The engineers are now doing their bit again, armourers fitting bombs and rockets, reloading as required, refuelling, then off again. We don't know at the time, but what is going on today is going to be the norm for the foreseeable future.

All the time we are getting an update of what is happening ashore on the islands, and apparently the Argies aren't happy. Well, they can bugger off home if they want to, then we can bugger off home also. The aircraft have been bombing Stanley Airfield and other areas within the Falkland Islands where the Argentinians are known to be. The good old RAF chappies (civilians in uniform) who had flown from Ascension, with, I believe, 21 1,000-lb bombs, were meant to have destroyed the runway at Stanley Airfield. Out of the 21 bombs, one managed to hit its target. That's not bad; 5 per cent success. Lt Cmdr Sharky Ward writes in his book that it cost £400,000 to carry out this task, which meant that it cost

£40,000 per bomb. He writes: "The FAA could have done it at a very much reduced price with more success." I tend to agree with him. As I mentioned earlier, in the FAA/Royal Navy we make it work; failure is not in our vocabulary. The FAA was actually formed before the RAF and was originally called the Royal Naval Air Service.

For the remainder of the day, this is the procedure: aircraft off, bomb their targets on the Falklands, return to 'Mother' (the ship), rearm, refuel, change crews, and off again, keeping the Argentinians awake and on their feet, tiring them out.

The crews on deck – the engineers, the marshallers, the armourers, the fire crews, the aircraft salvage team –has done their best and without incidents. It has been a very successful day on the *Hermes*, even though we are all tired and exhausted with the continual flying and the apprehension, stress and anxiety of what the pilots have been experiencing. Today, these young men became adults, looking after each other and their superiors.

My night shift turns to in our workshop in the hangar extension. I brief them on what has been happening during the day and what is required of them during the night, carry out routine inspections, and tasks on vehicles and equipment. The vehicles throughout the day had performed as expected, thanks to the team looking after them on the long journey south.

One day over. What is in store for the *Hermes* tomorrow? Probably much the same, operating outside the range of the Argentinian Air Force, but in range for our aircraft and *Invincible*'s aircraft to attack Argentinian positions on the Falklands. The Argentinian aircraft had to fly from the Argentinian mainland.

Time now for a dhoby (shower) and to wash out your nicks and socks. Doing this is a daily occurrence for sailors, unless you're a submariner! Then it's in for supper, before relaxing, but ready for anything; always having your survival equipment close at hand. It becomes part of you.

I notice, when I go to supper in the CPOs' dining hall, that the Leading Hand of the pot wash has started a 'diary' on the pot wash bulkhead. He isn't writing about the daily events, but is drawing the events, which start on the left-hand bulkhead just as you enter the pot wash. It is really good. I think that the whole of the bulkhead was covered in drawings when we got home.

The following day is much the same as the previous one. Up at the usual time, 0700-ish, into breakfast, watching to make sure nobody (visitors on the ship) is taking more rolls than they should. Sitting chatting with other CPOs; all of us wondering what today will bring. Then it's down to the workshop, fully booted and spurred (gas mask, anti-flash gear, life jacket, once-only survival suit, flight deck radio, etc.), meet up with the night shift, see how they have gotten on, everything left for them to do more or less complete; anything that wasn't, we, the day shift, will finish before it becomes hectic on the flight deck.

As the day progresses, we find out what the other ships of the Task Force have been up to. Our frigates and destroyers had been giving naval gun fire support all through the night. That's when the ships position themselves out at sea but close enough for their 4.5-inch shells to reach the islands; again keeping the Argentinians awake all night. When daybreak is about to start, the ships stop firing and make their way back out to sea and the safety of the ocean, putting a greater distance between them and the islands.

At nightfall, they return to a similar position and bombard the islands again throughout the night until the morning, then once again leave the area for the safety of the open sea. You can imagine it: the Argentinians not getting much sleep or rest, but, when you think of it, the crews on the ships wouldn't be getting much rest either, with these bloody guns firing all night and then closed up at action stations, where they would be fed by 'action messing': the food coming to you wherever your action station is. This procedure was to become routine until the day the Argentinians surrendered.

During the day, these ships would position themselves between the carriers and the threat from the Argentinians. They became the carriers' 'goalkeepers'. Other ships would be positioned some miles 'up threat', being used as an early warning system, warning the carrier group of any incoming threats. When a warning came, it gave us more time to close up to action stations, if we were not already closed up. Also to launch our carrier aircraft patrol (CAP): the Harriers that weren't being used to attack the islands. On an aircraft carrier, the ship's main armament is its aircraft. So, you can imagine, everyone onboard all of our ships was kept very busy and was always ready for the unknown.

Reconnaissance photographs from the previous day show several Argentinian aircraft damaged, along with areas where their troops laid low, around Stanley Airport and the surrounding areas and islands. I get this information during my visits to AMCO, when I go there to read the signals on a daily basis.

CHAPTER EIGHT

The Sinking of the *Belgrano*

~ • ~

Later in the afternoon of 3 May, at around 1600, it was time for 4 o'clockers with a cup of tea (but no cakes today as it isn't Tuesday or Thursday). I would have split my day shift so that there was always cover on the flight deck. In case of a problem or incident on deck, I was always only a minute or so away. The CPOs would gather in their dining room for a cup of tea. We would either stand or sit on the deck because all the tables and chairs had been stowed away and secured in case something happened, where they would be thrown around all over the place. They were brought out for meal times, then stowed away afterwards.

We were all sitting around, waiting on the World News at 4 o'clock. There was complete silence; no one wanting to miss a word. We wondered how the news came from London. Anyway, the news came on that HMS *Conqueror* had sunk the Argentinian cruiser, the *General Belgrano*, which was an old World War II cruiser. The silence was broken and a loud cheer went up, but, no sooner had it echoed around the dining room than the place fell silent again; everyone thinking of the poor bastards in the freezing waters of the South Atlantic, fighting to survive, not being able to save their ship – their home with all their belongings and shipmates still onboard – all trying to survive. After all, they were only sailors just like us, doing their job. It really affected us onboard, wondering if this was going to be worth it. Are we going to get home? When is it going to be our turn? All these questions start going through your head and in the back of your mind you're hoping that you survive.

There were more than 300 lives lost during this one action. It still haunts me to this day. I don't think I'll ever forget it. It could have been us, not being able to say your final goodbyes to your family and friends, being burnt to death, drowning. I hate the thought of it and I can understand how it affects individuals.

This was now becoming dirty. What else can happen? Surely, it is not going to be plain sailing? They, the Argentinians, are not going to take it lying down.

Tea over, it's back to work. The atmosphere around the ship is now solemn, everyone thinking about those poor guys in the water; hoping they get picked up soon.

After that incident, the Argentinian Navy hotfooted it back to their nearest base and never ventured out again, including their aircraft carrier *25th of May*, so now it was their 'air force' that we would have to be concerned about, along with their ground troops. Although, we still didn't know about their submarines. Were they still lurking about looking for our ships? We were depending on our helicopters from 826 Squadron, who were flying round the clock looking for submarines, keeping our ships safe. They did a great job. Rumour has it that they detected a submarine a couple of times, released their torpedoes and killed a couple of whales! You can imagine the mickey that was taken out of them by the other squadrons.

CHAPTER NINE

4 May 1982

~ • ~

The next day, 4 May, we, the Royal Navy, get our comeuppance.
It starts the same as yesterday, with no problems or incidents. The team is working well, the night shift has gone off to bed to rest before their next shift, tonight at 2000.

During the day, as usual, aeroplanes off, aeroplanes on, going about their tasks and missions with great success. The CAP aircraft are covering the carrier group, keeping us safe from above, and the helicopters are keeping us safe from below the waves.

But this wasn't to last. After lunch, the shit hit the fan. "Action stations, action stations, action stations!" Everyone now running to their positions, anti-flash gear on, night shift up and closed up below in our workshop.

One of our goalkeepers, HMS *Bristol* or HMS *Brilliant*, takes up their position, steaming alongside us, either on the port side or starboard side, depending on which side the threat is coming from.

Then we get the news: HMS *Sheffield*, a Type 42 destroyer, has been hit by an Exocet missile. Our helicopters are scrambled to assist. Not long after the news, the helicopters arrive back onboard with some of the injured. One guy was helped from the helicopter by two first aiders. His number 8 trousers look as if they have been blown off his legs and he has a wound dressing over his eye and head. Again, the Press is getting in the bloody way just for pictures. I ask my Leading Hand to go and assist with the stretchers. The answer I get, I didn't expect: "You'll be asking me to do brain surgery next!" I have to have a nice word with him!

Seeing and experiencing what is happening around us – after all, this can't be happening to us; we are the Royal Navy – in reality, is happening to us, and it is affecting people in different ways, and we have to look out for each other and help each other. It might not have been affecting people at that moment, but it is when you're alone and you start thinking about what has just happened, thinking about your mates on the *Sheffield*, hoping they survive. Thinking back, I can't remember seeing many officers about, although I'm sure they were. We all knew what to do and got on with it; we had practised it enough times.

The injured are offloaded from the helicopters and placed on the aft aircraft lift, which takes them down to a level where it stops, the armour-plated door opens and they are taken into the sick bay.

Once the helicopters are emptied, off they go again for more survivors.

In the meantime, some of our frigates are on the scene, helping, trying to extinguish the fire on the *Sheffield*. One of the frigates is HMS *Yarmouth*, which has Dave onboard, who I spoke to on the radio at Ascension Island. When we met up after this, he told me that they were alongside the ship, throwing cans of drinks to the survivors on the bow, while they, the *Yarmouth*, were fighting the fires and boundary cooling to prevent the fires from spreading from the outside. He also mentioned that the Chinese laundryman came out on to the bow where the other survivors were, then went back into the ship for his money and was never seen again.

In the end, their Captain, 'Sam Salt', gave the order to 'abandon ship'. He arrived on the *Hermes* a tired and weary man, totally dejected. Off he went to see the Admiral, and was then dispatched off the *Hermes* with some of the survivors on to a ship that would take them back to Ascension Island and onwards to the UK.

H.M.S Sheffield after being hit by an Argentinian missile.

It appears that when the *Sheffield* was hit, the ship's company weren't at action stations and in their main galley, and the deep fat fryers were still full of cooking oil (so I have been informed). The missile entered the ship through the side, into the main galley, setting fire to everything, and causing a fireball that ripped through the ship, destroying everything in its path. Once the ship was well ablaze, nothing could be done to save her, with many perishing.

Soon after this tragedy, my boss, Whato Whiting, came up to me and said that I was to get myself ready to be flown over to the *Sheffield* in one of the helicopters and see if I could salvage anything from the hangar. Fortunately, it was cancelled and I didn't have to go. They had changed their minds because the ship's magazines were still full and could blow up at any time. So to say that I was relieved is an understatement!

As I already mentioned, there were several of the crew of the *Sheffield* killed and lots more injured. They tried their utmost to save the ship, which is always the priority on a ship that has been damaged – whether in war or peacetime – but to no avail. It must have been an experience you couldn't relate to without it having happened to you. There must have been real acts of bravery: the ship's crew trying to save each other, along with trying to save their ship. It's different in the other services. Individuals can get injured but, on a ship, there are hundreds of personnel who can be injured or killed, just by one direct hit from a missile, rocket or bomb.

This had been a horrible day for everyone. Four days in and two ships lost, with hundreds of lives lost or perished. Who's next? everyone's asking. We have to stay focused, stay prepared at all times to expect the unexpected. Let's make sure we are safe and ready to help others or other ships that could have same unfortunate fate.

It has been a busy few hours. Once again, my lads have done their bit, along with everyone else. All that going on and the Harriers and Sea Kings keep flying. Now down to the hangar to tell the night shift to go and get some rest before it is time for them to come on watch to relieve the day watch at 2000. It doesn't matter if they are a bit late; we won't go off watch until they arrive.

Let's recap on what's been happening so far. On 1 May at 0700 GMT, a Vulcan bomber from the RAF arrives from Ascension Island, 4,000 miles away, and drops 21 1,000-lb bombs on Stanley Airfield. The Argentinians aren't expecting that. Once the Vulcan has completed its task, it heads for home; the Ascension Island mission complete. It's a good job that the media didn't know about this attack on the Falklands. If they had known, no doubt it would have been all over the newspapers, the cat would have been out of the bag, and the whole mission would have been a failure.

Now it's the turn of the Sea Harriers, from HMS *Hermes*. Each one loaded with three 1,000-lb bombs, they attack Stanley Airfield, along with the small airstrip at Goose Green, 120 miles to the west. The objective is to put the airfields out of commission, to close the air routes/bridge between the mainland, Argentina and the Falkland Islands. The islanders must have been pleased to know that we had finally arrived at the 'theatre of war', to start the task of removing the occupation forces.

On 3 and 4 May, the *Belgrano* is sunk, with loss of lives, hit by torpedoes from the submarine HMS *Conqueror*. HMS *Sheffield* is also hit by an Exocet missile, with loss of lives and also the ship, after the brave crew tried their utmost to save it until the Skipper gave the order to abandon ship. I can't imagine what it must have been like on these two ships. Fortunately, the *Sheffield* had other British ships in the immediate vicinity to help save the survivors.

The cruise ship *Canberra* is on its way with 2,000 troops onboard. It had called into Freetown on 18 April, for fuel and supplies, and to disembark the dockyard mates who had sailed with it to complete the modifications to the ship, for example, adding a refuelling point to enable it to carry out RAS, and to complete two helicopter landing pads. HMS *Invincible* was also successfully carrying out its tasks and mission.

One of our Sea King helicopters detects a small Argentinian vessel. It reports its position, and a Lynx helicopter sinks it with one of its missiles. The helicopter is then fired on by another vessel. It returns fire and damages it before returning to its ship because it is getting low on fuel.

So, the last four or five days had been a busy time for everyone, spending most of our time at action stations.

During normal routines, i.e. not at war, onboard Royal Navy ships, if you are off watch, not working, during the evening from 1730, you are required to change into night clothing (no, not pyjamas). As a senior rate, this is black trousers and a white shirt, either long-sleeved or short-sleeved. It was the same for all ranks, although now we can't remember the last time we changed into night clothing.

Once again, every day you see new faces onboard. Where they came from we don't know. The SAS and the SBS are now engaged in carrying out their top-secret missions ashore. All we know about it is when we see them going on to the flight deck and climbing into a Commando Squadron Sea King helicopter, with all their equipment, weapons, binoculars, fold-up canoes (that fit into their pockets), their faces covered in camouflage make-up (dark green), wearing woolly hats. I notice that they didn't wear any badges of rank; they all looked the same. Where were they going? What were they going to be doing? They are the only ones who knew; the pilots only knew where to drop them off. This is the task the Royal Navy and the FAA were designed for. It was important that we had to make it as safe as possible before the ground troops could be put ashore and then support them with naval gunfire and air cover.

The Task Force had been down there for nearly three weeks before the main ground troops went ashore. As I mentioned earlier, not everyone knows about the FAA, but it is older than the RAF and we are taught to make things work, because at sea we don't have the support that other military organisations have on land. At sea, you have to make it work to survive and be effective no matter where you are in the world.

But back to the South Atlantic.

There are some things that don't change, whether the ship is at cruising stations, exercising, alongside at a foreign port, carrying out defence watches or at action stations. If you're on the flight deck, you can tell the time of day by the smell, especially around lunchtime. The smell

H.M.S. Ardent assisting H.M.S Sheffield.

from the galley fan creeps over the deck and you can almost tell what's cooking. It really gets the taste buds going. Likewise, if you are on nightwatch/shift, just after 0400, say about 0430-ish and you're on deck, you know when the bakery has flashed up. The smell is unmistakable and you instantly know that there is not long to go before your watch is over and you can get your gnashers into one of those freshly-baked rolls, with either a slice of crispy bacon in it or a fried egg, or both, in the middle of it.

When we were down in the South Atlantic, some mornings, my PO, Nigel, would wake me at around 0700 with a cup of tea and a bacon roll. When this happened, I knew that all was well and that there had been no issues during the night. When I didn't get a roll, I started wondering, What's gone wrong during the night shift? Then you find out that there was nothing wrong. Although, one time, he came up with the tea and a roll and, as he left, he said, "There is no rush. See you when you come down." So I thought he must have had an easy night and was letting me rest a bit longer, or was he hiding something and needed more time to sort it?

As I ate my roll, the mind started wondering why and what's happened? So, I quickly finish my roll and tea, up and ready for work, and go into the hangar extension from the forward access door and into the workshop. Nigel's there and says, "Come with me." So, I'm thinking, What's up? We walk into the hangar and there in front of us is the Coles crane. "Nigel, what's wrong?" He says, "The cables f****d." "How and why?" He tells me, "One of the chock heads was using it and when he was lowering the hook he over sped the cable drum and the cable wrapped itself on the drum and, instead of lowering, it started going in the opposite direction, raising the hook." I asked him which chock head was it. He told me, so off I go to get a report. It transpires that he didn't have a weight on the hook, which would have kept the cable taught. He wasn't happy, and neither was I. I told him to not use the crane again and to get one of my lads to operate it in future. I then had to let Flyco know that the crane was unserviceable and that they couldn't fly until it was rectified. We had to change the cable, which took about four hours. Fortunately, this happened on one of our last trips and not while we were down south.

At this point, let me mention the different states that ships in the Royal Navy close up to. When alongside, you can make your way around the ship with ease: no doors or hatches on the main passageways are closed, apart from restricted compartments, for example, engine rooms and hangar accesses. When the ship is preparing to leave harbour and go to sea, certain doors and hatches are closed and clipped locked, for example, 'assume damage control state' and 'Y Yankee', so all hatches and doors marked with a 'Y' would be closed. The hatches on the decks have a smaller hatch in them. These are left open, so that you can go through them from one deck to the other. They are really just big enough to get normal-sized people through, so when you have your life jacket, survival suit, radio, gas mask, etc., it really is a squeeze, no matter what size you are.

When 'assume defence watches' is announced, this is usually the state the ship would be closed up to. The highest state is action stations when all hatches and doors are closed with all clips in the closed position. Even the smaller hatches on the larger deck hatches, so you can imagine the difficulty this causes moving about the ship with all your extra gear on. It's not so bad when you come to a big metal door, undo all the eight clips, go through, close the door and replace all the clips. But, the smaller hatches are a different kettle of fish. Undo the two clips, lift up the hatch, squeeze through with everything on, then close it behind you, and replace the two clips. Going up is not too bad, but going down, if you are not careful, it will crash down on your head, and they are not light. The purpose of all these heavy doors and hatches is to make the ship watertight. If it happened to be hit by a torpedo or a bomb, the sections of the ship that are affected can be closed off, giving the ship a better chance of survival and to carry on fighting, while the damage control teams get the chance to fight the fires or plug the holes or both. The rule is 'last man through the doors or hatches closes them behind him'.

With regard to the once-only survival suits we were issued with, which I mentioned previously, they were bright orange in colour and fitted like a Babygro, with the feet, body, arms and hood all in one. They were designed to give you protection in the icy cold waters of the South Atlantic or anywhere else in the world where they would be required, giving the wearer a better chance of survival and time to be rescued. Without them, your survival time would be reduced dramatically. The procedure relating to fitting your once-only suit is to put it on over your clothes, zip it up, then put on your life jacket. This way, you can inflate your life jacket and float. By putting it on the other way, i.e. life jacket first, then your survival suit, you wouldn't be able to inflate your life jacket and you would probably sink and drown. I hope this never happened to anyone.

We have been down south now for a few days. The weather is deteriorating by the hour and the sea state is rough most of the time. We experienced the four seasons in one day. With it being uncomfortable and 'lumpy', the aircrews were having to put all their airmanship skills to the test. We also had more Sea Harriers come and boost our complement. They had come down south on the SS *Atlantic Conveyor*. Some of their pilots had never landed on a pitching ship before, so the ship must have looked really small to them, but they made it without problem or incident, apart from one. I think the driver was an RAF chappie. He landed on a bit heavily, and bounced and landed with his port outrigger in the catwalk, so all hell let loose to get the lashings on to the aircraft to secure it to the deck. I learned afterwards that he RAF chappie (I say he was RAF because it wouldn't have been one of our professional FAA chaps, would it?) was considering ejecting. He climbed out of the cockpit on to the deck, all sheepish. Joking apart, it was good to see the extra aircraft arrive all in one piece, taking into account the size of the flight deck compared to landing on an airfield somewhere. Well done to all of them.

Fortunately, the weather on the day they transferred to the ship was kind to them, the sea was moderate, wind acceptable and good visibility. Well, if it hadn't been, it would probably have been a different matter. I'm not sure about this information, but there was a rumour that some of the aircraft may have flown down from Ascension Island.

One day, the area we were operating in was covered in a blanket of fog, which meant we could hide in it. Taking advantage of this, the lads were down in the workshop doing bits and pieces and drinking coffee. I stayed up on the flight deck, just in case. There were two Sea Harriers on the deck, manned up with the pilots, in a state of readiness. The pilots would sit in their cockpits for two hours at a time, then they would be replaced. They would be fully dressed in their flying overalls: immersion suits. These replaced their lightweight flying overalls and gave them more protection against the cold water if by chance they ended up in the South Atlantic. They would also be attached to their dinghy pack, have their flying helmet on, along with their life jacket, and would be strapped into their ejection seat, already to go at a moment's notice. The only thing left to do would be to remove the safety pins from the ejection seat, which is always the last thing to remove before flight, making the seat live. If required, the pilot could pull the 'D' handle, bringing a face guard over his face. The seat would then eject him from the aircraft, along with his dinghy pack. Leaving the aircraft in the air, hoping everything operates as advertised, parachute deployed. Land on land, brilliant; land on the sea, then your dinghy comes into operation along with your life jacket. The same with the dinghy, then it's, get into the dinghy as fast as possible, and pull over the skirt to protect you from the elements. Next thing you are hoping for is that your search and rescue beacon equipment (SARBE) is working, sending out a signal giving your position so that you can be rescued by either another ship or a helicopter from your Task Force; or anybody would be fine. Let's hope that the pilots don't have to experience ditching, although they would have practised it many times in the controlled environment of the safety equipment section of a swimming pool.

So, up in the island, I come across one of our Royal Marines. I think it was Staff Sergeant Mac Maclean. Like me, he was ship's company. The usual chat between us took place. "What's going on?" "How long do you think this is going to last?" We discussed all the new faces that keep appearing onboard, the next time we might receive mail, etc., bearing in mind that the mail from the UK would come via Ascension Island, then by sea from there to the South Atlantic, so, by the time we received it, it was probably a month old. (I think that I received mail only once from my sisters and brother during my whole time in the Royal Navy.)

While Mac and I were having a chat, one of the Press film crews were walking past. I asked them, "Why is it that you never take pictures of the guys onboard? Only pictures of things or events that are interesting?" They then asked us if we wanted our pictures taken. We said "Yes," so they did. If you go on to the web, look up 'The Voyage South HMS Hermes Falklands 1982'. I think that, after about seven minutes, just after Brian Hanrahan had interviewed someone, there are two guys wearing balaclavas standing on the goofing deck overlooking the flight deck and it's foggy. That's Mac and me. Our five seconds of fame.

During one of the aircraft launches, everything is ready to go, aircraft manned, engines running, lashings removed, armed up either with bombs or rockets, engineers clear of the aircraft, then I hear in my headset: "PO Cross (a Petty Officer Armourer), go and get your gun." I think, that's strange. I haven't heard that one before. I look around and at the top of the take-off ramp are four or five birds, either albatrosses or gannets, getting a lift or having a rest. A couple of minutes pass before PO Cross arrives back on deck with a shotgun. He walks up the deck towards the ramp, at the same time loading the shotgun, and slowly makes his way up the ramp, putting the gun to his shoulder. I hear in my headset: "PO Cross, don't shoot them!" Too late! Bloody feathers everywhere! In a split second, the ramp is clear and the aircraft can take off. So that was a bit of excitement. I reckon the birds had been trained by the Argentinians. Their air force couldn't find us, so they sent them to stop us from launching our aircraft!

Royal Marine and myself. Taken up on the island overlooking the Flight Deck.

CHAPTER TEN

Back to 'Normal'

~ • ~

Everything was now back to normal: aircraft off, aircraft on, hands to action stations, helicopters coming and going, hovering above the sea, listening for submarines. Visiting helicopters bring captains or other high-ranking officers onboard to have meetings with the Admiral; no doubt to discuss the developments and positions of the other ships and where they have to be and at what time. I can imagine the Admiral concluding his meetings by saying: "Thank you and good luck." Then they would probably take the opportunity to have a chat with the Captain of my ship to talk about certain issues, to help each other. Although they were from other ships, we were all in the same boat together, so to speak.

During our time down south, as a result of the constant heavy use of the flight deck, it was becoming unsafe and slippery with the wet, oily, greasy surface, and the flight deck tractors were losing their grip. On the *Invincible*, we heard that one aircraft handler, a young guy, had been crushed on their flight deck by one of the flight deck tractors.

All of a sudden, this brand-new pressure washer turned up in our workshop, to be assembled for use on the flight deck in order to remove the greasy surface. This machine cost £47,000, and you couldn't even drive it; you had to push or pull it. It produced 3000PSI of pressure, so, once we got it assembled and working, we presented it to the flight deck. The FDO, a Lieutenant Commander, was all excited about this new bit of equipment and wanted to be the first to use it, so, to keep dry, he put on his once-only survival suit and got to work. But the machine started controlling him. You could see his suit changing colour, from his feet up. As he got wetter, the further up his suit got darker with the spray working its way up to his hips. By this time, he had had enough and so it was switched off and given to a lower rank to use. It started with the FDO and ended up with a Naval Airman Handler operating it. Of course, they thought it was a new toy. Still it made our day, me and the team enjoying the entertainment.

It had been the usual day, with not much change to the routine of being at war. We had been at sea now for a few weeks, where we had experienced anything and everything that could happen. The day was over for me and my shift. I had handed over to Nigel and his team. So, it was shower, including washing your nicks and socks, then to supper, catching up with the others in the mess, discussing the day's events and any aircraft or ships that had been attacked and destroyed on both sides. We would also chat about the men and ships, stuck up 'Bomb Alley', getting attacked by the Argentinian Air Force, then the other ships inshore giving the usual naval gun fire support, all night, firing their 4.5-inch shells, getting no let-up or much needed rest or sleep.

We were lucky on the *Hermes*. Up till now, we were getting our off-watch rest and were able to sleep; albeit with one eye open and your ears listening out for anything unusual.

Some of the guys thought that it was safer to sleep in their workshops. They could have been right, because, as mentioned before, above my cabin on the flight deck was the forward ammunitions dump, so, if something kicked off there, I don't think we would have known much about it.

So, into bed to listen to some music, to take my mind of what was going on and the shipmates that had been injured or had paid the ultimate sacrifice. I would only use one of the ear pieces so that I could listen out for any emergencies, always thinking how long was this situation going to last, and how to ensure that my lads are okay, and getting them home where they belong with their families. I'm also thinking of my two children, hoping that I will see them again, and trying to put things into perspective, concentrate and always thinking about what could happen, hoping that I can cope.

I'm just settling down, then all hell lets loose and the shit hits the fan again. "Aircraft crash, aircraft crash, aircraft crash! Crash and salvage party to the flight deck." Straightaway I thought, it looks like Nigel and the team are going to be busy, then out of the tannoy comes, "Chief McDonald to the flight deck," which I ignored because I knew that Nigel could manage without me. Then "Chief McDonald to the Flight Deck at the rush!" I'm just getting up and putting my clothes and everything else on when the cabin door opens and there is Steven Ashford, one of the night shift, who says, "George, you're needed on deck." "I'm just coming, Steve. Thanks."

Now all your thoughts and concentration are gone. You are thinking, what's gone down and where? Let's get up there and assess the situation, hope no one has been killed or injured. You are surprised how many things go through your head in such a short time, when one minute you are just falling asleep, then this happens and you have to be wide awake and have all your wits about you, because all eyes will be on you, so you have to make the correct decisions and at the correct time, keeping your team safe, and that includes the aircraft handlers, who have now come into the equation, because they will be driving the flight deck tractors.

The time is now is 2300. I arrive on deck. It is pitch-black (darkened ship), so if there are any submarines in the immediate area they have less chance of seeing us. So, I'm on deck and along comes Whato. "Good evening, Chief. I didn't think you'd want to miss this. Situation so far. The aircraft is one of 826 Squadron. The ship is alongside it on the starboard side, by the ship's crane. So far, the crane is in position, the flight deck tractors are in position." Then he disappears. So, I go and find Nigel and we go and have a look over the side, and there it is, floating alongside the ship. Its flotation bags are inflated, keeping it upright and the sea state is perfect. The Sea King's fuselage had been designed so that it can, if required, land on water, although not something it did on a regular basis. Saltwater is not Sea King friendly. Come to think of it, no aircraft likes saltwater.

The lower part of the fuselage is shaped like a small boat's hull. So, the rotor blades have to be removed before it can be lifted. This means that the Coles crane is required. We then go and prepare the crane, start the engine and remove the lashings. I get in and start driving the crane to where it will be required with just the sidelights on and Nigel guiding me down the deck, when in my headset I hear music to my ears from Flyco: "Switch those f*****g lights off!" So now it is pitch-black again and I have to manoeuvre this big crane around parked aircraft, where there isn't much room for mistakes. To help, Nigel switches on his naval right-angle torch and starts waving it to tell me which way to go, to avoid hitting anything or damaging any of the parked aircraft, or run over any of the items in the ammunitions dump. As I mentioned, all eyes are on me, watching every move; that's if they can see me!

We have achieved the first part without any problems. Although it was carried out at a snail's pace, the crane is now in position, getting ready to bring one of the rotor blades up and onboard. After checking that the steadying lines are attached to stop it swinging about, it has taken probably one or two hours to get this far, when we get the order, which might have come via Whato from Flyco: "Cancel the recovery." The reason being that the helicopter has a live torpedo on it and they didn't want to risk bringing it onboard; it would be too dangerous. So now everything has to be done in reverse: detach the tractors from each other, remove all the lines attached to the helicopter, and return the crane to its parking area, with Nigel guiding me with his little naval right-angle torch, and lash it down.

The ship then gets underway, away from the crashed helicopter, which was then sunk. Now that I'm wide awake, I take myself down to the dining hall and have something to eat along with the night shift. I tell them they did good, which I knew they would. We have a cup of tea and a chat. As I'm going back to bed, around 0200, Nigel says, "No rush in the morning, George. See you when you're ready."

That is the sort of relationship we had with our teams, unless of course another emergency arose. I thanked him, told him not to work too hard, that I'd see him in the morning and to thank the lads for me, and with that, back to the cabin and into my little space: the middle bunk on the right.

Then your mind starts again, picking up from where you were four hours previously: the kids, your family, your friends, etc. You ask yourself, do I have to speak to any individual about their response to tonight's emergency? No, they did everything that was expected of them. They did everything as second nature; one of the best teams I have ever had. "Well done, lads," and off to sleep I went, happy as a lamb.

The week before we heard about the Falklands being invaded, the CPOs played rugby against the Officers (Wardroom). I was playing hooker and we got beaten 6–0, which wasn't a bad score. One of the officers, I was told, was an ex-England triallist and was built like a brick shithouse. I remember he came running down the wing with the ball towards me. I tackled him and went down like a bag of shit and was rewarded with one or two broken ribs. Although they seemed to be getting better, I just had to suffer in silence.

To make sure that all the ships' manpower and land forces were 'singing from the same song sheet', we were instructed to set all our clocks and watches to Greenwich Mean Time (GMT), so that there was no confusion with the time. Time now the same as the UK. I found this quite strange because we would go to work as normal at 0800 when it was pitch-black and wouldn't start getting light until 1130-ish, which was nearly lunchtime. On one particular day, as dawn approached and I was on the flight deck, as I looked towards the horizon I saw that there were ships everywhere, of all different shapes and sizes, all around us. Destroyers, frigates, landing ships, tankers, trawlers, merchant ships, mine sweepers, ferries. I'm sure that the *Canberra* was in among them. There must have been more than 50 of them; it was an awesome sight and a change from just seeing water or maybe our plane guard-come-goalkeeper. Then we were off again to the safety of being out of reach of the Argentinian Air Force, while giving CAP cover to all the new ships that had joined us.

I learnt that the *Canberra* had been anchored off Ascension Island for

17 days, waiting to receive information relating to where they were to go, or to disembark their troops on to the Royal Naval ships, HMS *Fearless* and HMS *Intrepid*, both assault ships. While they were at anchor there, the troops would go ashore on a daily basis to carry out live firing practice. It must have been a relief for them to know that they were not being transferred but would be carrying on their journey south on the *Canberra*. The reason, I'm led to believe, they didn't transfer was because both these ships were full to overflowing with other troops, so there was no room for the 1,500 troops that *Canberra* had transported from the UK.

Harriers from 800 Squadron had set up a Forward Operating Base (FOB) ashore; somewhere safe that had been checked out and secured by either the SAS or the SBS. This gave us a better advantage and cut down flying time from the *Hermes* to the islands. One of their engineers who went with them, by helicopter (another example of the FAA making things work!) managed to get a message back to me highlighting the fact that there was a shortage of drink at the FOB, so I managed to get a bottle of whisky sent ashore via one of the aircrew. I don't know if the engineers received it or not, but the thought was there. The conditions ashore must have been terrible because winter was now well on its way: cold, wet and windy, with the odd snowfall.

To help protect the Harrier aircraft and ships from incoming missile or rocket attack, the aircraft were modified to carry chaff, which was stowed inside the aircraft's air brake housing, fitted on the underside of the fuselage towards the tail. If there was a warning of an incoming missile or rocket, they would release the chaff, which, as mentioned previously, would give the incoming missile the impression that it was a larger target and so it would aim away from the aircraft and miss its target.

On one occasion, the flight deck was working like clockwork, everything was going smoothly, the Sea Kings taking off and returning, doing rotor running refuels and crew changes, then off again to their designated areas to listen for any Argentinian submarines that might be brave enough to come anywhere near us. The Sea Harriers had been airborne and were now returning to refuel and rearm. I, as usual, positioned myself at the bottom of the ramp, where I could see down the deck what was going on. The Harriers would fly towards the ship just above the flight deck level along the port side. When they reached the required position for the spot they were going to land on, the aircraft marshaller (in his yellow surcoat) would instruct the pilot to go into the hover and then bring the aircraft to starboard over the flight deck, to over its landing spot, where he would land vertically on to the deck and shut the engine down. On this occasion, all the aircraft had landed and shut down, but I could still hear the sound of an engine running very close to me. I turned around and there was a Harrier. It had landed on the ramp, facing downwards, so I immediately went up to the nearest aircraft handler and tapped him on the shoulder to let him know that there was one behind him. It appeared that the pilot had just made it back to the ship before running out of fuel. I met up with him years later at a charity dinner. When I told him the story, he confirmed that it was him. I said, "You bastard! You nearly killed me!" We had a laugh about it, and a beer. It was good catching up with you, Bill, who was by now a Commodore.

More new faces appearing on the ship; you never seem to see them arriving. This bunch were from the SAS or SBS and had arrived from Ascension Island to carry out a special operation: to fly to mainland Argentina and destroy their Super Etendard aircraft that they were using to deliver Exocet missiles. They had flown down in an RAF Hercules transport aircraft and I believe had parachuted into the icy cold South Atlantic and were picked up and brought to the ship by boat. Onboard, one of the Commando Squadron helicopters, a Sea King Mk4, was being modified and prepared to fly them to the mainland. All unnecessary equipment was being removed to make it lighter and it was being adapted for inflight refuelling. They were to go that night but it was rescheduled for the following night; the reason being – so I was informed – that they were tired after their long flight from the UK to Ascension, then on to the Task Force. Also, they didn't know what a Super Etendard looked like, so they used the extra time to rest and brush up on their aircraft recognition. The crew for the task were volunteers: a pilot, an observer and an aircrewman. This operation was kept from the journalists, so that it wouldn't leak out; not like some of the previous operations, when they were so eager to beat each other with a story and send it back to the UK, where it would become public and be dispatched through the BBC World Service, etc. It was with issues like these that the Admiral was going to ban all information that the Press was sending back to the UK. It was getting serious: the Argentinians were getting the information on what we were doing before we heard it on the news onboard.

The helicopter took off 24 hours late. The distance to the mainland was more than 1,000 miles, I believe, at night. There were ships stationed along the route to enable the aircraft to carry out inflight refuelling and this was done because the flight deck on the smaller ships wasn't big enough for the larger Sea King to land on. Refuelling was achieved by the helicopter hovering above the small flight deck and lowering its winch cable down. The team on the ship's flight deck would attach the HIFR to the winch, which was then hoisted up, brought into the cabin of the

Harrier ready for launch at a minutes notice.

helicopter and attached to the modified refuelling point inside the aircraft. Once the refuelling was complete, it was disconnected, all in reverse order. Then off the aircraft would go on to the next ship. I think that this was carried out three times.

When the aircraft reached its destination, which was the Argentinian Air Force base close to Chile, the special forces deployed the aircraft with all the necessary equipment, plastic explosives, etc., did what was required of them and then disappeared into the night. That is what I'm led to believe occurred. Meanwhile, the helicopter took off and flew over into Chile, landed on a remote beach and the crew disembarked the aircraft, set fire to it – to make it look like an accidental crash – before making their way into Chile, staying low for a while before giving themselves up to the Chilean authorities.

It's always nice to meet one of your old mates. I was on the deck as usual, when I hear in my headset, "Standby to receive a Wessex 3 helicopter from HMS *Glamorgan.*" Although from Glamorgan, this aircraft's parent station was Portland in Dorset, where I had been based, so I'm waiting on it to arrive to see if I know anyone onboard. The aircraft lands on, the cabin door slides open and out jumps 'Spider Kelly', a Petty Officer Electrician. I served with Spider in 737 Squadron, when I was their Line Chief. I go across to him for a chat and the first thing he says to me is: "Mac, what the f***k's going on? This isn't nice or healthy!" He tells me that the SMR of his flight was an old pal of mine, David Lee. I ask him to give him my regards and also ask if they need anything. We have a coffee and he is off again back to his ship, which was doing lots of things close to shore. I tell him to keep his head down and to wish Dave and the rest of the team onboard good luck. That was the last I saw Spider but I know that he returned safely.

Like all the other ships of the Task Force, their crews didn't know when they were going to put their feet on dry land again. We weren't even thinking about it; all we wanted to do was get on with the job in hand to the best of our ability, then think about going home to our families and standing again on terra firma. The meals hadn't changed; still the same rationing. The veg was usually broccoli and broad beans; none of the popular peas, carrots or cauliflower.

With all that was going on, along with the chit-chat about where we were, what we were doing, where we were going, things that were happening throughout the ship and what was probably happening on all the other ships, we would sometimes talk about things that were the norm when not at war. A good example was 'Saturday Night at Sea'. This was an unwinding period in the Chiefs' mess and probably other mess decks throughout the ship. It happened no matter where we were, anywhere in the world, at sea or alongside. It usually started around 1800, when the bar would open. Then there was cocktails available: 'Harvey Wall Bangers', 'Black Russians' or 'Tom Collins'. They used to cost 50p a go, so some Chiefs would fill a pint glass and it would last them most of the night. At 1830, it was supper time in our dining room. Usually something nice, like steak, egg and chips. Remember, we had the chief caterer in our mess, which was a bonus. After supper, it was back in the bar to unwind, having a general chinwag, telling jokes, and laughing about things that had happened on the ship, probably at someone else's expense. Later in the evening, Taff (Chief Aircraft Handler), would get his guitar out and we would have a sing-song: sea shanties, folk songs, rugby songs, etc., where we would all join in. We also had another guy – I think he was an electrician – who played the trumpet. The only thing was, he could only play it while reading the sheet music, so one of the other Chiefs would have to hold the sheet music for him while he played, while dressed up for the occasion in a black cape. The only trouble was, the guy holding the music couldn't read music, so didn't know where he was on the page. He would also just carry on drinking his beer. When he got to the end of the page, the trumpeter would let the guy know by raising and lowering his trumpet, but that only worked if he was paying attention and not drinking his beer and chatting to someone. It was very funny; tears would roll down grown men's faces and they would choke over their beers.

A similar night was called 'Up Channel Night'. This was carried out the night before we would enter a port or return to our home port (Portsmouth harbour). The ship would anchor for the night just off Portsmouth, to the south of the Isle of Wight. As I mentioned, these were times when we would unwind and relax. We could have been away from home for over a year, so it was nice to see the coast of Great Britain once again. These are naval traditions, that have been going on for years and years. I hope that they carry on for many more years to come.

When the ship was alongside in Portsmouth for any length of time, we used to encourage the families to come onboard for Sunday lunch, which again was good fun, and we would show them that there was another side to being at sea. They would come onboard, have a drink and then lunch. Mums and dads would go back into the bar and catch up with others while I would take the kids up on to the flight deck and let them have a go at driving the flight deck tractors – under supervision of course – which they all enjoyed and it gave their parents a break, albeit for a short time.

As I've mentioned previously, there were six of us in my cabin – two AED Chiefs, two engine room Chiefs and two squadron Chiefs – so when the squadrons were ashore we had much more room in the cabin. My bunk was the middle one on the right as you entered, the top one belonged to one of the engine room Chiefs and the bottom one was for one of the Squadron Chiefs. The guy on the top bunk above me was an engine room watchkeeper, working four hours on, four hours off, so when he was off watch you would keep out of the cabin so that he could rest, but at night when he came in at around 1230, or 0430, or get up to go on watch, nearly every time my leg would be in the way as he placed his foot on my bunk when he got out of his.

Down in the South Atlantic, they had constantly been watchkeeping without a break, which they would normally get when the ship went alongside somewhere, but not now. It must have been really stressful for them being stuck down in the engine or boiler rooms, knowing that all the hatches they had come through were now closed behind them, wondering what was happening on top. The only clue they would have was whatever the ship was doing: turning hard to port or starboard, increasing or decreasing speed, or doing both together. Getting the news about other ships in the Task Force, through the normal channels, from the bridge or

Falklands 1982.

damage control headquarters, of ships being attacked, damaged and even sunk, wondering if it was going to happen to the Happy Hermes, when it would cease being happy, that was the feeling throughout the ship, no matter where you were on it. When we spoke about each other's action stations, they said that they would prefer being down below than being on the flight deck with me. I preferred it the way it was.

We had another visiting aircraft from my old mate and neighbour's ship, HMS *Yarmouth*. This was the ship that had had a problem with its HIFR gear, that I spoke to on the ship's radio while at Ascension on the way south. Who steps out of the aircraft and on to our deck, in his flying overalls and flying helmet, but my old mate Dave. He seemed pleased to be onboard for a visit, and we went for a coffee and a long chat. I was updated on what his ship had been up to, and was glad that I was on the *Hermes*. He told me that everyone on the *Hermes* had qualified for the West African medal because we were so far away from the action! (cheeky bastard!). We had a laugh about that. The *Yarmouth* had been in Bomb Alley, giving naval gun fire support, helping survivors from HMS *Sheffield*. They were also one of the ships that had gone close enough so that they could throw cans of drinks on to where the lucky ones were gathering on the fo'c'sle, so that they could have a drink to clear their throats. Although Dave was pleased to be visiting us on the *Hermes*, he looked really tired and I asked if I could get him anything. I think he ended up taking some books, bread and a selection of cheeses. Don't ask where it came from; I just know that he appreciated it. We still talk about it now every time we meet. Once he had everything onboard and the purpose of the visit was over, as usual I said, "Take care, buddy, and keep your head down. See you back in the UK." He then climbed back into the helicopter and was off, and we gave each other a wave as he went into the unknown and more danger.

The news comes in "The first of the land forces have now landed". They had been taken in by the SS *Canberra* and transferred to the landing crafts from HMS *Fearless* and HMS *Intrepid*, more or less during first light. The SAS and SBS had done their jobs in making it as safe as possible, finding out where the highest risks were and doing their best to eliminate them. With what had been going on at sea, we knew that they were going to have to put all their training, skills and professionalism to the test; not only to fight but to beat the weather also. The weather had deteriorated terribly, with snow, sleet, wind, rain, freezing temperatures, and it was going to get much worse. Poor sods! At least we on the carriers were warm and reasonably safe, albeit still not knowing what was lurking under the water, or over the horizon, or when or where their aircraft would come from. We all knew we were prime targets and were closed up at emergency/action stations nearly all day. But those poor bastards on land had it bad although the Navy did their best to support them. After all, we had been at sea for nearly a month prior to the land forces arriving, so we were used to the weather out at sea, which could change by the hour. Believe me, it did change. The waves would become mountainous, breaking over the bows of the carrier, making it roll and pitch all over the place.

I receive a message one morning from the flight deck that one of our flight deck tractors had tried to escape, so off we leg it to the flight deck, to find one of the tractors hanging over the round down (the aft edge of the flight deck, which curves downwards, removing the sharp edge. It was designed this way for when the ship was a conventional carrier, with catapults and arrester wires. If the aircraft came in too low, it had a better chance of survival and of keeping its undercarriage intact). So here was this tractor trying to escape; probably had had enough! Fortunately, the driver had managed to apply the handbrake and leap clear. Good thinking. I would have hated to explain why we had a tractor missing, and, if the driver had gone over the arse end, I don't think he would have survived the waters of the South Atlantic or the fall of about 40 to 50 feet into the water, which had a heavy swell at the time. He also didn't have his survival suit on, which you would only put on if you knew you were going to go into the water. It was still dark and daylight wasn't until around 1100. Fortunately, someone had been quick to attach some aircraft lashings to the tractor, preventing it from going any further. Since it was still dark, we weren't at flying stations, which was in our favour because we had time to recover the vehicle by attaching other tractors to it, along with our crane, and pull it back on to the deck. Therefore, no explanation to the boss necessary, although he did want to know how it went. "Okay, Whato, Sir."

When these situations occur, there is no written procedure to rectify the situation. You have to use your experience to the best of your ability and do a risk assessment as you tackle the task; something you are taught in the Royal Navy.

A liquid oxygen tank was due to arrive onboard by Chinook helicopter as an underslung load, from the *Atlantic Conveyor*. It was mid-afternoon, things on the flying side were quiet and we needed to get this rather large container on to the ship because the *Hermes* was running low on oxygen supply. The LOX, as it was known, was used for the Harrier pilots and was required for them to breathe above 10,000 feet.

We had decided that, when it was on its way, it would be lowered on to the port aft quarter of the flight deck, near to where the tractor had tried to escape, which was the area where the downwash from the Chinook's rotor blades would cause less damage, if any. The tank was delivered without incident, even with the deck pitching up and down in the heavy swell of the South Atlantic. As soon as we could, as soon as the container was over the deck, we got heaving lines on to it to steady it, which wasn't easy because the down draught was hell-bent on trying to blow us over the side.

The Chinook returned to the *Atlantic Conveyor*, which left us with the task of moving the tank to forward of the ship's island. This turned out to be a slow process, especially with the pitching deck, because we had to use the Coles crane. So, once it was lifted clear of the deck, it would start swinging from side to side, even with steadying lines attached. When it got too bad, and before it took control, it was lowered back on to the deck to steady it again, then we would start all over again, eventually getting it to its final resting place, where it was lashed down securely.

You have to realise that health and safety along with risk assessment on a warship is common sense, and that you should talk to the team about what they think is the best and safest way to carry out tasks. With the ship's movements, one minute you're going one way, the next you're going the other way, then uphill, then downhill. You have to anticipate what the ship is going to do next, usually by watching the waves, and, if the ship is going to alter course, sometimes you can get caught off guard, which can be quite stressful and worrying, because you don't want to damage anything or any aircraft or worry about causing injury to anyone. You have to remember that you are not the only one on the deck; it is a very busy and dangerous place, and there is no room for error, so you just go at a very slow pace so that you know that, if something goes wrong, you have time to correct it or stop whatever you're doing.

The inside of a warship is not like a cruise liner; the only similarity is that it floats on the water. The interior is a bit cramped, the junior rates are accommodated in mess decks, which hold from 10 to more than 50 persons. The smallest mess I was in when I was a junior rate was 24 persons and the largest was 78, when I was onboard HMS *Ark Royal* in 1963 as a 17 and a half year old with 800 Squadron, which had Scimitar aircraft. There were only beds around the mess square (where we all sat and relaxed, when not working) for 13 persons. The rest of us had hammocks, which, when slung properly, was like sleeping in a banana

The escaping tractor.

skin. Well, that's how I imagined it would be like. Messes have no carpets on the floor, the decks are tiled and polished and there are these big, heavy metal doors and hatches. The distances apart depends on the size of the ship, and the hatches allow access to the deck above or below.

Pipes and electrical cables are not covered up; they are in view throughout the ship, and are marked for what the pipes are carrying: 'Fire Main', 'Water', 'Furnace Fuel Oil (FFO), 'Aircraft Fuel', etc. Every so often, you come across damage control equipment stowed on the bulkheads, which includes timbers, splinter boxes and aqua torques. Then there are the firefighting appliances: fire hoses (2-inch for inside the ship; 4-inch for exterior), plus fire extinguishers, water, foam and CO_2. There are lockers with breathing apparatus in and first aid stations, with their Neil Robertson stretchers hanging on the bulkheads. These are for strapping in casualties so that they can be moved around the ship by hand and taken safely to the hospital. Then there are first aid boxes throughout the ship. These stations are located on all decks and are in view of everyone, so, if required, people can get to them quickly. In an emergency, every second counts and, when not at war, first aid procedures are practised every day, including 'Man overboard' exercises. You never know when you are going to hear "For exercise, for exercise, for exercise! Fire, fire, fire in 3A4!" (3 Deck Alpha section compartment 4, junior rates galley) or "Fire party close up at the rush!" Then all you hear and see are the required personnel to fight the fire rushing to the scene with their equipment. So this happens on a daily basis. It's important because the priority is to save the ship, no matter what, then your shipmates.

I now get word that my divorce has come through, so my mind is elsewhere. Will I get back to see my kids? What am I doing? I must try and concentrate on the job in hand and not do anything stupid, and put it to the back of my head, which is difficult. Tomorrow's another day, so it might be easier then, I think, and hope.

One early evening while having supper, the eventful happened: the klaxon sounds three times: "Hands to action stations, hands to action stations, hands to action stations! Incoming air threat. All hands close up." It is a quick grab what you can from your plate and go, leaving the pot wash team to do their duty, clearing away all the tables and chairs and stowing them away safely, so that if anything happens they won't obstruct the emergency parties carrying out their tasks. Everyone is now automatically putting on their anti-flash gear while stuffing whatever they have in their hand into their mouths, not knowing if this is going to be their last meal on the *Hermes*.

When action station sounds, the atmosphere on the ship changes instantly. One minute, everything is reasonably peaceful – everyone carrying out their tasks and duties to the best of their abilities – then all of a sudden, without warning, the klaxon sounds three times, calling **all** onboard. The atmosphere has changed instantly, from a peaceful ship cruising along, to a fighting warship. All you hear is the footsteps of personnel running up and down ladders and armour-plated doors and hatches slamming closed. These separate and secure the sections fore and aft of the ship and the decks above and below. Then you hear all the clips being turned into the closed position. The crew are putting on their anti-flash hoods and gauntlets. You can tell who is who by their name tag on their overalls because all that is visible are their eyes through the slot on their anti-flash hoods. Once everyone is closed up, there is silence, apart from the sound of the ship, the buzz of machinery, the odd door or hatch being opened then closed, then the clips.

Everyone is now in their own 'bubble' of deep thought, wondering, Is this our turn to be hit? Will I survive? Am I ready to do what I have been trained to do? Where is the best escape route? Where is the nearest first aid post? Are my mates okay? Is the team ready if need be, to fight a fire, stop flooding? What if the lights go out? There are a thousand things you have not been trained for, including coping under the stress and pressure. God, I hope so! Everyone is relying on each other to survive whatever. Will I see my family again? My brother, sisters, mum, dad, kids? People pray to themselves for strength and to be brave, no matter what. Everyone is tense, just waiting for whatever is going to happen. All we wanted to hear was the 'all clear' and relax; only until the next time, which could only be minutes away. "Klaxon, klaxon, klaxon! Action stations, action stations, action stations! Enemy aircraft detected from the East! Footsteps on ladders, door hatches closing, clips on, etc.

RIP those on both sides who gave the ultimate sacrifice. One would have been one too many.

The Argentinians were now using the tactic of coming in under the radar screening that the ships were putting out. They would drop down below the radar screen and fly at low level, popping up for a second or two to check where we were, drop back down again, then, when we were in range of their weapons, they would come back up to release them, drop back down again and away, returning to the mainland. Fortunately for us, the British forces, they were releasing their bombs at too low a level, which didn't give the necessary time for the bombs to fuse or arm themselves, which meant it was like dropping a 1,000-lb brick. Although it didn't go off, it still did a lot of damage and, unfortunately, with the ones that landed on ships, some exploded during the process of being

Rescuing the escaping tractor.

disarmed by the bomb disposal team, who paid the ultimate price. They are a brave lot.

The pot wash picture diary was now down one side and about halfway along the next wall, showing pictures and drawings of the Argentinian aircraft that had been shot down, the *Santa Fe*, their submarine that had been attacked and damaged, the *Belgrano* being hit, showing the little orange life rafts in the water, the fishing boat being attacked in the TEZ, and of our ships – a sharp reminder of where we were and what was happening around us – *Sheffield*, the *Coventry*, the *Achilles*, the *Sir Galahad* and the *Ardent*. Again, we were thinking, when will it be our turn? and you just pray for your mates that didn't survive on these ships and the Argentinian losses. We were all sailors; it doesn't matter what nationality they were. Then again you think of the job in hand, keeping your team safe and doing your best, hoping that the decisions you make are the correct ones, and not forgetting the families back home and the children.

We are all now thinking, I hope it's over soon and the worrying back home will stop one way or the other.

Then news comes through that on the *Ardent* someone I worked with in 771 Squadron had perished. The FAA is a small force compared with other military outfits, and you start to realise that you mustn't become complacent or cocky. Everything you do has got to be 100 per cent, and you must have faith in your ship and its crew, being prepared to do whatever at a minute's notice, whether it's helping to save your ship or shipmates; not worrying about your own safety. Everyone onboard now is thinking, we are losing too many ships and shipmates on those ships that have been destroyed. What is happening now is going to affect all of us one way or another for the rest of our lives, if we survive. You think of all the ways to survive if your ship is hit, what to do as quickly as possible, then, will I survive the cold and freezing rough seas of the South Atlantic? Only time will tell whether you are put into these situations, hoping and praying that you're not.

We hear the news that the *Canberra* is going to South Georgia to bring the troops off the *Queen Elizabeth 2* to keep well clear of the troubles at the Falklands. After all, we can't let Cunard's precious boat get its paint scratched! The troops it was transporting were the Welch Guards, the Scots Guards and the Gurkhas. I learned afterwards that the Welch Guards had more suitcases with them than you would take on a world cruise, changing clothes every night, plus they had brought the regimental silverware and disco equipment (they had a strange way of going to war). The *Canberra* then had to take them to the Falklands and drop them off ashore to reinforce the ground troops that had already landed. From what we were hearing, the troops ashore were having a hell of a rough time making ground and were waiting on the big helicopters to be brought ashore from the *Atlantic Conveyor* to help them move forward, bringing the heavy guns, etc. with them. The *Atlantic Conveyor* was in our company most of the time for protection.

The guys onboard the *Hermes*, and probably all the other ships, were becoming tired by now, not having had proper sleep and rest since leaving Pompey. They had endured more or less everything that could possibly happen, including mountainous seas and gale-force winds. The sea would crash over the flight deck at times, the aircraft and equipment would need to be double lashed or more to keep it attached to the flight deck. It was uncomfortable enough for us on the *Hermes*, so God knows what it was like on the smaller ships, getting thrown all over the place, holding on all the time, not sleeping in fear of getting tipped out of your bunk. All you wish for is calm seas, where you can make your way along the passageways without bumping into each other, or knocking into the bulkheads, and, at meal times, the gravy not running into the custard, and vice versa. Although, once you get used to it, you just think, well, it all goes down the same hole!

At times, you could semi relax, for example, when carrying out an RAS, which was usually every five to seven days, taking on aviation fuel and ship's fuel. The ships would steam to a safe area where the Argentinian Air Force couldn't reach them, plus it was usually carried out under the cover of darkness and took maybe four or more hours, depending on the sea state. Once complete and all the lines between the two ships were let go, we would be off again, bringing the ship into range, so that our Sea Harriers could carry out the support required for the ground forces ashore, along with their CAP duties.

The ice cream parlour had now been out of operation for quite a while. There had been no time to open it; also, the stock was low. So, thinking if and when we are on our way home, I'll need stock, I came up with this brilliant idea: send a letter to the *QE2* and the *Atlantic Conveyor* and see if they have any spare. This helped to take my mind off things, so I did, and waited and waited, but no such luck. So, it stayed closed.

Now everyone is just carrying on with routine after routine, thinking, what can I do to change it? You would do silly simple things like go a different way to work or use a different heads (toilet). You would think of all that which was out of routine or the ordinary (if you can call being on a warship 'ordinary'!).

CHAPTER ELEVEN

Air Raid!

~ • ~

I had worked out that the Argentinians didn't come out to play after 1700-ish, so this particular day I decided I'd go down and have an early shower since it was quiet, rather than wait until my usual time of 2000. So, off I go, leaving my leading hand at the helm, letting him know where I would be. I go to my cabin and strip off, collect my dhoby gear and towel, then make my way to the showers. Great! Peace and quiet, all to myself. Nicks and socks washed, teeth cleaned and shave carried out and into the shower. Lovely jubbly, I thought. This is the life! Just what I needed to relax and destress myself. Then – you've guessed it – the klaxon sounds: "Hands to action stations, hands to action stations, hands to action stations! All hands close up! Air raid warning red!" I thought, these f*****g Argies have changed their tactics. Bollocks! So I grab my towel and dhoby bucket, and I'm off back to my cabin, starkers, then I hear someone shout, "George, you forgot your anti-flash gear!" I thought, no matter what the situation is in the Navy, there is always some comical bastard! Into the cabin, overalls on, no nicks – no time to put them on – grab everything else and make my way to the deck, putting my anti-flash gear on as I go.

On the deck, I quickly assess what's going on, go into the ACR and speak to Lt Jim Bradley, the ACRO. He puts me in the picture. Then I go back on to the deck and make my way to behind the island, where our salvage locker is and the rest of my team; we are all there. I look out to sea. Our goalkeeper is in position sailing alongside us, on the starboard side, about 50 to 100 yards away, at the same speed as the *Hermes*, between us and the threat. Also, I notice a large cargo ship with black smoke billowing out of it. I think, they are having to burn a lot of fuel to keep up with us. I reckoned it was about three to four miles away off the starboard quarter; it might have been closer. Then I hear activity in my headset. I think, what the f***'s going on? The SAR helicopter is scrambled, then it comes over, "The *Atlantic Conveyor* has been hit." I think, Jesus Christ! That was meant for us! Now it's getting too f*****g close for comfort. The SAR helicopter comes back. I look up and all I can see is that it is full. When I say 'full', it was standing room only. It must have been overloaded (all up weights were not adhered to during these times) with survivors in their bright orange dayglo once-only survival suits. It has to fly around because there is no room on the deck for it to land. A space is quickly made available and it lands and the occupants jump out. Once all are out of the chopper, off it goes again to pick up more survivors.

When I see the survivors, I think, bloody hell, it's the repair teams from MARTSU! I immediately go over and speak to them and ask, "What happened?" "The ship has been hit by an Exocet missile." "Are there any others from MARTSU?" "Yes, they are onboard fighting the fires." So, I give them my bar number and take them down to the Chiefs' mess, and tell them to have whatever. Then I make my way back up to the flight deck just in time to see the chopper return with more survivors; again, with some more MARTSU guys on it, who I also take down to the Chiefs' mess and reunite them with the others.

The next load brings the guys who have been fighting the fires. One is on a stretcher; some have to go straight to the sick bay, which is accessed directly to the flight deck via the aft aircraft lift, taking them down to the sick bay level. Access is through a big armour-plated door into the hospital. The sides of the liftwell are painted black. It's your duty to help these guys. As the lift is lowered, it is like going into a big black hole or a bottomless pit. I check the guys in the mess, before going to the sick bay to see the guys there, who had inhaled smoke and required treatment, to see if they needed anything. It becomes personal when you come across guys you have worked with in the past, and you feel it's your duty to help them in whatever way you can.

Now, back on deck. The only Chinook helicopter that, fortunately, was airborne at the time that the *Atlantic Conveyor* was hit, now had nowhere to go because they had abandoned ship (another ship lost, with loss of life). Through my headset I hear the order, "Make room on the deck for one Chinook helicopter; it has nowhere to go," so, again, everything on the deck is set into motion to make space for a large helicopter. Sea Harriers are hitched on to tractors and moved to a safe area, along with the Sea King helicopters. Eventually, there is enough space made available so that this large helicopter can land. I don't think it stayed for long because it was required ashore with urgency to help the land forces advance.

There were four Chinook helicopters lost on the *Atlantic Conveyor*, along with vital equipment for the land forces. The MOD learnt from this, I hope, not to put all their eggs in one basket.

The following is an account of that day, which I found on social media several years later.

'On the British side, all hell let loose, as ships tried to down or distract the incoming Exocet missiles.

The small frigate, HMS *Ambuscade*, which was passing across the track of the missiles, didn't have weapons capable of shooting them down, but was able to launch chaff. HMS *Brilliant*, which did have suitable weapons, was able to continue tracking the missile, but was unable to fire her Seawolf missiles as she was too far away.

The Captain of HMS *Hermes* ordered full power to race ahead of the accompanying *Conveyor* and RFA *Regent* before turning the ship sharply to port to bring her bow round to face the threat, as had previously been agreed with the planners in London. There was confusion on *Hermes* as the ship heeled into the turn. *Hermes* was armed with antiquated Sea Cat missiles, which were also not capable of destroying the Exocets, but she fired chaff towards her original position in an attempt to confuse the missile.

On *Conveyor*'s bridge, Captain Ian North's team and the helicopter pilots watched the warships firing chaff, and heading off in various directions. As the *Conveyor* was not fitted with any defensive weapons or chaff launchers, her only defence against missile attacks was to turn her stern towards the incoming missiles and use the thick stern ramp as a makeshift armour plating. The turn would also minimise her radar profile and place the bow magazines of cluster bombs and deck fuel tanks as far away from the likely point of impact as possible. However, *Conveyor* wasn't fitted with military radar capable of detecting the attacking missiles, so her command was totally reliant on being informed of the threat direction by accompanying warships.

Unbeknown to her command, *Conveyor* was at this point almost stern on to the incoming missiles and therefore already in her defensive posture. But another order came through from HMS *Hermes*, on the permanently manned "tactical" channel, for *Conveyor* to immediately turn to port, on to course 040 (as recorded in the Board of Inquiry report). The civilian Master, Captain Ian North (who died in action), ordered the turn, which, when completed, would have maximised *Conveyor*'s visibility by placing her exactly side on to the incoming missiles.

RFA *Regent* was presumably also ordered to port by the flag ship on to a course that took her astern of the *Conveyor*. As recorded in Admiral Woodward's log, *Conveyor*'s naval party Captain, Mike Layard, hurried to the bridge from the mess decks far below and tried to find out the direction of the attack from the flag ship, but to no avail.

Hermes, meanwhile, had now put *Conveyor* between her and the missiles. In addition, whilst *Hermes* was rapidly reducing her radar profile by turning towards the Exocets, *Conveyor* was increasing her visibility by following *Hermes*'s navigation instructions.

At about six to eight miles out from the destination set at the launch, the Exocet missiles switched on their seeker system to find *Hermes*'s current position. The missiles hunted ahead looking from left to right to find the largest surface target within a pre-set escape distance from *Hermes*'s original co-ordinates. By this time, *Conveyor* had become the largest target and the missile turned away from *Hermes* towards her.

Less than a minute later, the Exocets emerged from the smoke ball behind *Ambuscade* and witnesses on the *Conveyor* and surrounding ships observed both Exocets slam into *Conveyor*'s port side, punching holes right through her. Those on *Hermes*'s bridge were even able to make out the markings on the missiles as they came in. The Exocets spilled their burning propellant through *Conveyor*'s open inner decks, igniting her inflammable cargo and the ship quickly filled with acrid thick black smoke. The engines stopped and the smoke got into the ventilation system,

Atlantic Conveyor after being hit by Exoct missile.

quickly spreading it round the ship and out on to the decks, impeding the damage control parties.

Conveyor's crew fought a heroic but ultimately futile battle to save the ship, whilst *Conveyor*'s escort, the frigate HMS *Alacrity*, came alongside to play hoses on the decks. But the fires continued to spread and the *Conveyor*'s upper decks were soon cut in two by thick black smoke.

Eventually, *Conveyor*'s crew abandoned ship. Some were picked up by helicopter from the bow, while the rest took to the freezing sea, where many found their survival suits filled with water. Later, *Conveyor*'s bow magazine exploded, sinking the ship.'

Twelve members of *Conveyor*'s crew, including Captain North, perished on that day. RIP.

The following are some comments as it happened.

LM: Ian _____

"I was off duty. me, Mo Morris and Wacker were hot bedding. I was just in me pit (*bed*), when it came in… I thought, f**k! Six days before my birthday…bloody typical… So, I wrapped myself in all the bedding I could grab and sat amongst it with other chaps in the mess… Then hell broke loose above us and I thought that's it… but slowly it passed and I made it out. Six days later, best birthday I have ever had, they even made me a cake."

FW: "I was in the Wardroom galley under a table shitting myself."

JH: "Was on watch in the ACR. Remember the ACRO diving under the desk as I manned the phones."

PD: "On the flight deck ready to launch the Harriers when all hell broke loose. Will never forget it. RIP shipmates."

BH: "We actually saw the Exocet fly down the length of the flight deck."

CK: "I'd just put a Sea King on to 3 spot, by the lift. Swear to God, I thought I saw something flash past the bow. If I remember, told the FDO, who just said, 'You may have done'."

JR: "I never saw any of it. I was locked in B engine room lying flat out on the deck plates as they piped 'Stand to' over the machinery space tannoy. I was shitting myself. It still makes me cringe."

It had been a long day, so, once I have handed over to my trusty nightwatch, I go into the mess and have a beer with my old mates and shipmates from MARTSU, who are now getting over the initial experience of what they had just gone through, although it will take many years to fully get over it, if they ever get over it. Also, I visit the sick bay to check on the others there.

They weren't with us for long; they were transferred to another ship. I do know that some were landed ashore to carry out battle damage repairs to some of the aircraft. Knowing the experience and knowledge of these guys, the aircraft would have been repaired, just to make them safe and airworthy to continue supplying the men ashore and the ships. Also, to carry out casualty evacuations (CASVACs) at short notice, bringing the injured back from the front line and delivering them to the nearest hospital, whether it's the field hospital (probably an old cow shed or outbuilding) or one of the ships with an operating theatre, either *Canberra, Uganda* or even the *Hermes* or *Invincible*. The helicopters ashore were the troops lifeline. Now that there was only one Chinook helicopter left available, this put more stress on to the ones that were already ashore. Not only the helicopters but the ground troops. They were relying on the big helicopters to move them forward on their advance to Stanley. Now there weren't enough helicopters to do that. But being the professionals they were, this wasn't going to stop them. It was decided that, due to the circumstances and running out of time because of the weather deteriorating minute by minute, they would walk ('yomping': walking while eating) and fight their way to Stanley.

When we heard of this onboard, we thought, it's 40-odd miles in freezing cold weather, snow, ice, fog, rain – you name it. They must endure it along with freezing temperatures and putting up with trench foot problems. Let's hope they make it and, most of all, survive both the elements and the battles ahead of them.

CHAPTER TWELVE

Aftermath

~ • ~

On the *Hermes* and the *Invincible* it was much the same as each day passed. We would watch the aircraft take off into the miserable weather, the pilots on their own in this little fibreglass bubble, sitting on a seat that, if required, in a split second, and by pulling on the yellow and black handle, he would be propelled out off and cleared of the aircraft (the ejection seat included his dinghy pack, with all his survival equipment inside; also his parachute). The next step would be the parachute deploying and he would be clear of his ejection seat and he is now hoping that, when he lands in the water, his dinghy is going to inflate so that he can climb in before he's frozen to death or his balls have dropped off. Once the pilots have taken off, we are always anxious for their safety and their safe return. When they do return, the aircraft is prepared for the next sortie and it all starts again, with us once again hoping and praying for their safe return.

After days and weeks of this environment, pressures and stress, it does affect you mentally, where you don't really sleep properly at night, waiting to hear the news from around the fleet and from ashore. All we were wanting to hear was that the Argentinians had surrendered and that it was all over. Once the *Atlantic Conveyor* had been hit, it was brought home to all of us on the carriers that they could get through the defensive screen and get us, so we must be prepared for anything at any time.

Now that my divorce had come through and with what had been happening around the fleet, with ships being sunk and mates perishing in those icy cold waters of the South Atlantic, or in fires that had broken out within the ships (their homes) that had been unfortunately hit, I was becoming confused myself. Although legally I was single, I still had my kids; they were mine and no one else's. I would lay in my bunk, thinking and thinking, what am I doing and what to do until I was exhausted and just drifted off, but these thoughts were still there in the morning, until I got to work, when I had to focus on the job in hand, which really was an escape from my personal problems, until the time of day came when

HMS Plymouth departing for home passing down starboard side of Hermes.

I was alone again and my mind started all over again: kids, shipmates, family, who are worried about you as they sit at home watching every news bulletin. You try to clear all these thoughts from your mind when you're alone by listening to music (with one ear listening for the next "Action stations", "Fire onboard", etc.); the other ear tuned to Neil Diamond, Barry Manilow, Barbara Streisand, but it doesn't always work. When is this going to be over? For some, it is already over. Completely. What are their families, friends and shipmates thinking? Not only us but what about the Argentinians, who are having the same nightmares?

We get news of the RFA *Sir Galahad*, with the Welch Guards onboard. What were they doing onboard? We thought they had been put ashore. The ship was at anchor after bringing the Guards round from where they had been originally put ashore. It was carrying ammunitions and the Argentinian Air Force detected the ship and bombed it; receiving a direct hit. The Guards suffered a great many casualties and more than 40 deaths. The sister ship to the *Galahad*, the *Sir Tristram*, was also hit. When we saw the footage of the outcome – seeing the survivors in the lifeboats, with the Sea King helicopters of the FAA on the scene immediately, hovering in positions to blow the thick black smoke away from the lifeboats and trying to help blow them towards the shore – we felt for those poor bastards, fighting for their lives to get ashore, where the troops there were helping, some up to their waist in the freezing cold water.

Once again, the feeling throughout the Happy Hermes wasn't happy. You could tell what everyone was thinking just by looking at them: When is it going to be our turn? Let's get this over with once and for all.

Four days later, on 12 June, early in the morning, as day breaks, HMS *Glamorgan* is hit. My first reaction is, "Oh shit!" Spider Kelly and an old pal, Dave Lee, are on there. I hope that they are alright. In the mob (Royal Navy), we are all close; it doesn't matter where or what ship you're on, we are family. Things you were thinking of back home are now erased from your mind and you are just thinking of these poor buggers on the *Glamorgan*, fighting to save their ship and shipmates. You wait and wait to hear the news in more detail, then it comes through: nine killed. The Exocet missile had hit the hangar as the ship lent over in the turn at speed, which reduced the height of the ship's side, bringing the hangar closer to the water. Then I get the news: Dave, the ship's flight SMR didn't

HMS Plymouth and HMS Glamorgan leaving for home.

survive the attack. I have to go somewhere quiet and be alone, gathering my thoughts, and I can feel tears running down my face. "I don't know if I can take any more news like this." I start cursing the Argentinians, Maggie Thatcher, the Falkland Islands – which I had never seen in my life and didn't really care about. My list of mates is being reduced because of an island 8,000 miles away from the UK. They, the unfortunate ones, will never be going home ever again, I'm thinking, to see their families, kids, loved ones, mums, dads, grannies, grandads. The list is endless.

Again, the ship is in mourning, not much being said. One of our Chiefs on the *Hermes* has moved his bed down into his workshop because he thinks he will be safer there. No doubt there were others thinking the same. As for me, I thought often about the munitions dump that was directly above my cabin, but you then forget about it. War is a horrible experience; it plays on your mind every second of every day and no doubt for the rest of your life, if you survive.

We get news the following day that the land forces have seized Mount Tumbledown and other key positions and are closing in on the capital: Stanley. On the ship, the mood is changing once again. The aircraft,

Stanley after the surrender, June 1982.

the Harriers, are busy giving air support as always, but it seems to have intensified. On the *Hermes*, we feel and hope that it will end soon, one way or the other. Then the next day, 14 June, we get the wonderful news that we have all been waiting for. The stress, the worry, the sleepless nights will become memories. "White flag flying over Stanley." I immediately think, why the f**k couldn't they have got there two days earlier and my list of mates would have been longer.

Although we have heard the news, it isn't time yet to relax. We keep up with the air support and cover and hope the news wasn't fake news. So, everything stays the same, until it is confirmed.

CHAPTER THIRTEEN

Homeward Bound

~ • ~

The news that follows the next day, 15 June, is, "The British forces have entered Port Stanley."

I must say it was a strange feeling, hearing that announcement, after being at sea for so long in all weather conditions, and, now the hostilities were over, we, the British Forces, had been successful in what we had set out to do: to liberate the Falkland Islands from the aggressors. But at great cost, financially and in the human loss of life, on both sides, 8,000 miles from home. What an achievement! Overcoming all the issues that we encountered.

We stayed at sea in the area, still being on high alert, not dropping our guard.

After a while, it was announced that some of the ships would be leaving the area for home. The first of them approaches us from astern on the starboard side. We stand on the flight deck and watch it sail past. Their bridge has sandbags around it; the Captain and other officers and crew are standing on the bridge roof waving and holding red flares in their hands. The Captain salutes as they sail past, with their firehoses throwing up jets of water, the decks lined with sailors with huge grins on their faces, relieved that it is all over apart from the voyage home to their loved ones and families. We, the survivors, are the lucky ones.

Then comes the turn of HMS *Glamorgan*, which affects me deeply. I am standing on the flight deck just aft of the island, alongside Commander Barry, when the *Glamorgan* sails past, just as the others did, looking weary, rusty and tired, and it shows that she has been at sea for a long time in these rough and unforgiving waters of the South Atlantic. As she makes her way along the starboard side and the aft section comes into view, we see the hangar; the damage caused by the missile is covered up by a tarpaulin. My immediate thoughts are of my mate and his family, and I have tears in my eyes. I look at Commander Barry and he is also very emotional. I have never forgotten seeing these images and I don't think I ever will.

We get news that the Argentinian prisoners of war have been taken off the islands on the *Canberra* and one of the other ships – it might have been the *Uganda* – and have been taken to Puerto Madryn, in Argentina. Also, that some of the land forces are now being embarked on ships and are on their way home. We also hear the news that we, the *Hermes* will be going home once HMS *Invincible* has carried out some repairs and servicing, which pleases us no end. I don't think the guys on the *Invincible* were very pleased though. We, on the now Happy Hermes, felt really sorry for them!

One of our final tasks is for the ship to anchor in Port William, which is just outside Port Stanley, so that the islanders can see us and let the Admiral and his staff disembark, so that they can be flown back to the UK. So, we make our way slowly into Port William and, as the islands get bigger and bigger, we can see the outline of the mountains, Wireless Ridge, Two Sisters, Tumbledown, Longden, etc., along with Port Stanley. Up till now, they had been only names to us. Eventually, as we get even closer, we can make out the little red houses with their corrugated tin roofs spread out along the shoreline, with the cathedral in among them.

Our anchorage at Port William is quite far from Stanley. We can't see any of the inhabitants or locals, but I'm sure they can see us through the snow, which had started falling that afternoon. The helicopters make a formation flypast with the White Ensign fluttering beneath one of them, and fly along the shoreline of Stanley, which must have been a magical sight and a relief for the islanders, knowing they had been liberated and were now free of the Argentinian occupying forces.

We didn't stay long. Now that the Admiral and his lackeys had left the ship, our Captain Linley Middleton (a great man) had the ship all to himself, with his crew. We may have only been at anchor for about four hours before weighing anchor and turning around and heading out to sea, after just a glance at what it had all been about. The reaction onboard was a mixed one: was that it? It just looks like Scotland or Wales! Who would want to live on somewhere like that? The islands disappeared behind us in our wake, getting smaller and smaller, with every revolution of our screw. This was the first and last time that the *Hermes* and her gallant, exhausted crew would see land until we arrived at Ascension Island on our way back to the UK, and home.

The *Invincible* was now ready to take over from us, after it had completed its repairs and servicing. As the other ships had done before leaving for home, now it was our turn to transfer anything and everything we could spare on to other ships that were not due to leave the area for some time. To carry this out, once again, the helicopters were busy, not only still looking and listening for submarines – even though they had surrendered – but also now transferring stores. However, we now knew that it wouldn't be long before we would be turning north and starting the 8,000-mile voyage home, with the sun rising on the starboard side and setting on the port side, just in time for the last days of summer, to enjoy them with our families and loved ones, and my two great kids.

I'm still confused, with lots going on in my head, on what to do, since I was now single. Dave and Allan's families keep coming into my head, and I'm thinking, those poor kids didn't ask for this and what is there future going to be like without their dad?

Eventually, we get the long-awaited announcement that we will be turning north and heading for Ascension Island, but we will still carry on at our state of readiness, carrying our survival gear with us at all times, which we don't mind as long as we don't hear the pipe for action stations, and don't have to wear our anti-flash gear (which had been all nice and white and clean and smelling of mothballs when we first had it issued, but now it was dirty, worn and smelt awful. I think that if you dropped it on your foot it would have damaged something!)

The guys were now starting to relax a bit. You could tell by the expressions on their faces, although deep down they were thinking of their mates that weren't going home. You have to be a member of the very close family, the Royal Navy, which includes the FAA and the Royal Marines, and not forgetting the Submariners, deep down under the waves. There is no other military outfit that has the same camaraderie as the Navy. We work hard together, play hard together, live together and look after each other, onboard the ships. Also, when you go for a run ashore, making sure your oppo gets back onboard on time and safely.

Not long after turning north for Ascension, there was a pipe over the ships tannoy: "Will 847 Squadron personnel report to the Regulating Office." I thought, that's strange because we don't have any 847 helicopters onboard. The word got around, so I'm led to believe, that somehow, they got onboard and were hoping to get home, even without their helicopter! So, I think they were flown off the ship, back to wherever their aircraft was. Jack will try anything to get home!

The journey north was more relaxed than it had been for the last four months, when we were preparing the ship for the passage south, going to war, carrying out what was necessary and required of us, working long hours, and coping with really rough seas with mountainous waves and freezing cold weather. As we progressed north at a steady speed, 826 Squadron were still carrying out their anti-submarine role and the Sea Harriers were still flying because the aircrews had to keep their flying hours up to keep them 'on their toes'. On an aircraft carrier it never stops; it is always active. The ship itself was now getting back into its normal routine, carrying out exercises on a daily basis: exercise fire, exercise crash on deck, exercise steering gear breakdown, etc.

The temperature is now rising, the sea calmer, as we leave the roaring forties, and the flight deck is becoming more and more available for recreation because the flying is less intense. People are coming on to the deck from within the tin box of the carrier. Some have been stuck in there for weeks, only seeing a glimpse of daylight as they made their way across the weather decks, so they are determined to get a suntan before they get home, so out come the shorts of all different shapes, sizes and colours. It makes a big change to what the activity on the deck has been over the past four months; the guys on deck looking out for each other.

My guys were great. They performed outstandingly, with only a couple of hiccups, which I put down to the environment we were in and the stress it caused, and this goes for the night shift also, under the great leadership of Nigel.

Going on to the flight deck early in the morning before everything starts is awesome. After having been inside the ship all night, coming out into the fresh air is something you can't explain; it's so nice. Once out on the deck, all you can do is just take in the view, which is unobscured

RAS – taking of fuel in the South Atlantic.

all the way to the horizon, listening to the sound of the ocean as the ship ploughs through the mass of water on her way to her next destination. As I mentioned before, if you happen to be out there during the early hours of the morning, you can tell that it has gone past 0400; the time when the morning watch in the bakery starts making the daily requirement of bread, and the aroma of the baking bread filters up and over the flight deck. With that and the darkness of the sky, highlighting all the stars up above, it's such an overwhelming sight and place to be. At times, you wouldn't think you were on a warship. You are there alone in your thoughts, until it all starts again, with "Hands to flying stations".

Now it is getting warmer as we near the Equator and we start to see the dolphins once more, along with the flying fish, the odd shark and even a whale blowing as we get further north.

We knew we were getting closer to Ascension Island, which was coming into range for the heavy Chinook helicopters. I could see one flying towards us; it must have been a weekday because I had been told that the RAF don't work weekends! The helicopter flew around, waiting on permission. Because of the size of its rotor disc, it took up a lot of room on the deck. When it eventually landed onboard and shut down, the rotors stopped rotating, the front access door opened, the steps dropped down, and out came this RAF chappie, in a light brown, short-sleeved shirt, with matching light brown shorts and sandals, carrying his camera. He then gets himself into the correct position and starts taking happy snaps, until the FDO sees him. I couldn't help but laugh. This poor chap got the biggest bollocking of his life, before disappearing back into the helicopter, after the FDO has requested him to "get off my f*****g flight deck!" During flying stations, it is a must that you are dressed correctly. You must be covered up at all times; you never know when there might be a fire or crash on deck.

I believe that some companies in the UK donated gifts for the guys down south on the front line, but these never made their way to us; they only got as far as Ascension Island. If this is true, I hope that the authorities don't have a clear conscience. They had no idea what the guys ashore were having to endure.

Another couple of days and we will reach Ascension Island. On the way, we have carried out the usual and regular RAS, maintaining our dwindling supplies along with fuel. As we approach Ascension, we hear that some of the squadron personnel are flying back to the UK. Initially we think they are the lucky ones, but when we hear why, we know that they are not so lucky. They are to be disembarked on to the island and then flown home to the UK, probably to Yeovilton RNAS or RAF Brize Norton and bussed to Yeovilton. They will have some leave and, on completion of their leave, they will prepare other aircraft, Sea Harriers, and get them ready to embark on to HMS *Illustrious*, the Royal Navy's brand-new aircraft carrier. Once onboard with all their aircraft, Harriers and Sea King helicopters, they will carry out the usual operational readiness inspection (ORI). I say 'usual', because all the Royal Naval ships have to do this every so often, especially after major refits. Once the ship and crew have passed their ORI successfully, the ship can become operational and will set sail for the South Atlantic to relieve HMS *Invincible*, so the guys who were leaving at Ascension wouldn't be home for long before going back down south.

The next day, we would be anchoring off Ascension, so, as mentioned previously, it was a good chance to start the old tradition again of 'Up Channel Night'. That day, the helicopters were bringing on stores as underslung loads. There were all sorts of things coming onboard and, when we recognised the items, we thought that we were home and dry. There were salads, lettuce, tomatoes, cucumbers, etc, that we had not seen for weeks, maybe months. Then we heard that food rationing was to cease and that we could stand down from 'state of readiness'. Great news! No longer having that continual fear the had been hovering over us, for what seemed forever. The worry, the stress, the anticipation of when was it going to be our turn. I can't put into words what that moment meant to everyone. It was such a relief. Maybe we will be able to sleep properly now and my nightwatch will be able to join us on days, where we will be a full team once more. Also, they may be able to get a suntan before we reach the UK.

With that news, it meant no longer having to carry our survival equipment around at all times, doors and hatches could be opened up, and mess decks below the water line could now be occupied, which must have been wonderful news for those guys. They could get back into their messes on a permanent basis and sleep in their own bunks instead of some quiet corner of the ship. The 826 Helicopter Squadron was also no longer required to carry out anti-submarine patrols, but, best of all, there would be chips on the menu, which meant that it really was true: we were standing down from the readiness state. Having chips on the menu meant that we could all put a bit of weight back on, because we had all lost quite a bit, not only because of the food rationing but also through concern and worry. So, now there seemed to be only good news for most onboard, apart for those that weren't going home, who had to prepare for their next draft on HMS *Illustrious*.

So, at 1800, in the Chiefs' mess, was cocktails to start off Up Channel Night. Everyone (except those on watch, either running the ship or down below in the engine and boiler rooms) was now in their night clothing (for the first time since leaving Ascension on the way south), consisting of black trousers and white, short-sleeved shirts, ready for a good evening. Nearly everyone from the mess was there to let their hair down (the officers called it 'high spirits'; we called it 'getting pissed') after such a long period of stress, lack of sleep and worry. The ship's company's CPOs, 800 Squadron CPOs and 826 Squadron CPOs were all there. It started off with great humour and atmosphere. We all had supper – with chips – then it was back into the mess to carry on with the laughter and consumption of numerous glasses of ale, rum, cocktails, etc. You name it, we had it! Our mess manager had made sure that the bar was well stocked for the evening ahead.

At about 2130, the two squadrons started on at each other, with 800 saying that they were the best and 826 not agreeing with them. Then 800 mentioned that the only hits 826 had had were a couple of whales (they thought they were submarines). The ship's company Chiefs were laughing and egging on the two squadrons; it was becoming quite heated. When I went to the heads (toilet), I was standing there doing my business and minding my own, when one of the 826 Chiefs came in, moaning like hell about 800, and saying, "Who do they think they are? We (*826*) have been flying around the clock for weeks and months! They are really pissing me off!" Now, me being diplomatic and understanding – and a negotiator – I mentioned that there was a firehose outside the mess door. "Go and soak them! That will make you feel better." I went back into the mess and said to my mate, Mo, "Watch this." In came the other guy. I can't remember how far he got, but I do remember the mess president shouting, "The bar's closed!", so, if anyone remembers the incident, I'm truly sorry. It then went quiet in the mess and everyone started chatting and wishing those who were flying home all the very best and well done and safe flight home, see you back in the UK, take care, thanks, etc.

The next day, the guys flying home disembarked. We were now at anchor, so the flight deck was open for recreation. I was in the hangar saying my goodbyes to guys who, like everyone else, had been through thick and thin, with memories that would haunt them probably for the rest of their lives.

While at anchor, there was a remembrance service for the guys who weren't coming home. One of them was one of our pilots: Lt Nick Taylor. The service was held on the flight deck over on the aircraft side lift. The padre had a wreath that had been sent out from the UK. It was quite an emotional service, which was well attended by people from nearly all the ship's departments. We had a minute's silence before the wreath was cast overboard into the sea. In the bay where we were anchored, there were several other ships anchored. No doubt, their crews felt the same as us: relieved to be going home and that there was not going to be any further unnecessary deaths.

We didn't stop at Ascension for long before we started the final part of our remaining 4,000-mile journey home. Every day brought us closer, and the atmosphere onboard was becoming more and more happy. Unfortunately, there were those onboard who still had to carry out their watchkeeping duties: in the engine and boiler rooms; on the bridge; in the galleys; and in the radio and radar rooms, etc. No matter what operational state the ship was sailing under, these departments carried on regardless, so, when in your mess deck or cabin, you always had to consider the watchkeepers (something you were taught and learnt soon after joining the Navy: always consider others). Now that all the doors dividing each section of the ship were open, along with all the hatches between each deck – returning the ship to normal – it certainly did make it more enjoyable being onboard this magnificent warship, that had looked after us and was now taking us home; although she looked tired and overworked, just like her crew.

Everything was returning to normal. Even the ice cream parlour was opening once again, after a period of being 'closed due to other commitments'. A routine pipe was made from the bridge: "The ice cream parlour is now open and will remain open until 2100." So now back to normal. Where did the last few months go?

I had more or less made up my mind that my children must come first. I didn't want them to not have a dad around, like the poor kids whose fathers weren't coming home. It was an easy decision to make. It's strange when you're at sea. I would go to bed early, unless there was an Up Channel Night or Saturday Night at Sea going on, because I thought that the time would pass quicker. So, as usual, get to bed – your own little space – and listen to your music.

We are well on our way now. The meals onboard have really improved since we brought fresh produce on at Ascension. Now we were getting chips on a regular basis, which means that the deep fat fryers are operational and that rationing has ceased. We have also picked up sack loads of mail, so everyone is happy, apart from those onboard who have received 'dear Johns'. To have a happy sailor, all it takes is to keep him fed, along with mail on a regular basis, although he's not that keen on writing letters, if the truth be known.

The ship is now battering its way up through the Bay of Biscay, which eight times out of ten is a bit uncomfortable – rocking and rolling, pitching and tossing – but nothing compared to what we had experienced down in the South Atlantic, so it doesn't bother us; we just take it in our stride.

By this time, the squadrons' aircraft and their personnel are preparing to disembark on our return to Portsmouth, but they have been informed that they will not be flying off until after the ship has docked because we are expecting a tremendous welcome home. After hearing about the welcome that other ships have experienced on their return, the squadrons didn't want to miss this once-in-a- lifetime event, so this means that they will experience it twice: once in Portsmouth and the other when they return to their parent air station (Culdrose for 826 and Yeovil for 800 and 845 Commando Squadron with their Bootnics [Royal Marine Commandos]).

As we get closer, it is becoming even more relaxed onboard. During lunchtimes, I notice odd events happening. Some guys are carrying holdalls as they move along the passageways to their cabins. I think, that's strange, they must be changing cabins. But, on closer inspection, I see that the holdalls' contents are rectangular boxes. Put two and two together and you realise it's a crate of beer! So, immediately, I check out which cabin they are making for and decide to let them get started before I knock on the door and get an invite; and it worked!

When we were on passage up the English Channel out of sight of 'Guz' (Plymouth), all of a sudden, a frigate appeared. It was from the Dartmouth Training Squadron (Dartmouth College is the Royal Navy's officer training college, where they are taught to take charge of sailors. They don't know what they are up against!). The ship sailed towards us and, as it got closer and closer, we could make out the crew standing along the guardrails in Procedure Alpha positions. It was a great sight. As they sailed past, they all started cheering the mighty *Hermes*, and waving. I'm sure that they would have loved to have been part of what we had achieved. It was a very emotional moment. We then started waving back to them. It made us realise that we were nearly back home.

The news we were now getting from home was a minute-by-minute report of where we were and when to expect us alongside in Portsmouth, our home port. The ship now had to be made ready for being tied up alongside and for our return; something it had not done since leaving in April.

As we got even further up the English Channel and closer to Pompey, we got news that the new carrier, HMS *Illustrious*, was out on sea trials in the same area we would be passing through. When we got word that it was close, the majority of our crew made their way up on to the flight deck to see this new ship. And there she was! All new, shiny paintwork, making way at speed, she was coming more or less straight at us, then, all of a sudden, at about half a mile away (probably closer), she turned

Memorial services on the flight deck of H.M.S. Hermes whilst anchored off Ascension Island.

sharp to port, heeling right over. It was a very impressive sight. The flight deck was full of cheering sailors waving to us, just like the frigate that came out from Guz had done. I recognised an old mate, Geoff. You may ask, how could you make someone out from that distance? Well, it was quite easy actually. You see, he was a Chief Chef, so he was the only one wearing whites and he had his cap on. The rest were either in their number 8s – blue shirt with dark blue trousers – or overalls.

Now we knew that it wouldn't be long. Nearly there.

While making our way east, along the English Channel, there came an announcement over the tannoy, which went something like this: "Please pay attention. This is the Commander speaking. Any persons onboard that have in their possession any Argentinian weapons of any description, it is illegal to land these ashore, so I recommend that you dispose of any such weapons before we reach our destination." I think that this was directed towards the Royal Marines because these were the only ones who had been ashore on the islands with 845 Squadron; I don't think we had any SAS or SBS left onboard by this time. I can imagine somewhere in the Channel that there are a few Argentinian rifles or pistols lying on the seabed.

We were all starting to wonder what kind of reception the old tug was going to receive once we approached the dockyard, but before this was going to happen we would all have to clear Customs, which I thought was a farce. After all, the majority of the crew hadn't been ashore anywhere, but that's Britain for you. For this to happen we would be anchoring once more, overnight around the back of the Isle of Wight, and the ship would be darkened; no lights visible from shore.

It was time to position all the aircraft on the flight deck because, for Procedure Alpha, they all had to be in their exact spot, the same distance apart. The flight deck tractors also had to be in their places, so that, from looking from above, everything was uniformal. The last time we had done this was when we had departed and set sail for the South Atlantic, not knowing how long we would be away for or whether we would be coming home. It was to become 'The Journey to the Unknown'. Well, we had been there and had carried out the impossible with the aircraft, ship and equipment we had available, but unfortunately at the expense of too many lives on each side. The ships and aircraft lost could be replaced, but the lives **never**. Was it worth it? Well, it depends on who you ask. More about that later.

We have now reached our anchorage for the night. The aircraft have been positioned for entering the dockyard: Procedure Alpha. On the side of the ship's island, aft of the bridge, looking out to starboard, a scoreboard has been painted, showing how many Argentinian aircraft and ships were destroyed or damaged. Unfortunately, each one meant that their occupant or occupants had probably been killed, leaving a family fatherless or a mother without a son.

We hear that the Prime Minister is coming onboard in the morning for a visit, but will be flying ashore before we weigh anchor and set sail on the very last leg of our journey. After sailing to the South Atlantic and back – 16,000 miles – plus operating there for weeks and months, we have only between 10 and 15 miles remaining until we tie up alongside in Portsmouth. The excitement onboard is increasing by the minute. What is it going to be like? Will there be anyone there to meet us? How long will it take before we can get off the ship?

The working day is nearly over, and it is nearly time for Up Channel Night. Everyone is excited about tomorrow – the day we have all been looking forward to, ever since we left in April – but first it is time to relax with mess mates and reflect on what you've done and been through, including what will tomorrow be like and who will be there. The Captain didn't want anything cleaned or painted on the battle-scarred old girl. Let them see what we experienced. After being in some really mountainous seas, the ship's hull is covered in streaks of rust, running from below the flight deck. Everywhere you look it is a brown colour and caked in salt. It looks a sad old boat, on the outside, but on the inside, it is happy. She has done her bit and brought her crew home safely, but both are exhausted.

Up Channel Night started just like all the others had started, in all other parts of the world previously visited, throughout the ship's long, distinguished life since the 1950s. The guys who had finished their work for the day had showered and had changed into their night clothing. The junior rates would be doing the same and getting stuck into their daily beer allowance (plus the beer they had stashed away ready for tonight; the beer would have been hidden anywhere and everywhere as long as the ship's 'Reggies' (police) couldn't find it. How do I know about this activity? You must remember that the majority of senior rates were themselves once junior rates; it was a naval tradition.

Everyone onboard now is getting even more excited by the minute. It might have had something to do with the alcohol being consumed. There is even laughter heard within the ship, which is a good sign, because we know that tomorrow when we meet up with our families and loved ones there are going to be questions and more questions about our experiences, the memories will come flooding back, and it will be difficult to mention or explain what you have been through without getting emotional, which is going to last for a long time, if not for a lifetime.

In the Chiefs' mess, the CPOs are now gathering and having a drink – maybe a beer or a cocktail or a gin and tonic – before going for supper at 1830. For many, it will be their last supper before going ashore tomorrow. Also in the mess are the Chiefs from the ship's company who had been flown home from Ascension to take leave, but have been flown back onboard so that they can experience coming back home on the ship. The Skipper didn't want anyone to miss it. Also, they will be able to man the ship while the rest of us get some well-deserved leave.

Supper over, it's back into the mess. We have certain rules in the mess, which is the same on all ships: what is said or happens in the mess, stays in the mess. Officers were only allowed in the mess at lunchtimes, and by invitation. Everyone is now feeling relaxed, enjoying a drink. Taff, the Flight Deck Chief, gets his guitar out and we have a good sing-song: some country and western, some old sea shanties, some rugby songs. At 2100 (9 o'clockers), we have some bits to tuck into. Normally, we paid 50p for this; on the Up Channel Nights or Saturday Nights at Sea, the money collected went to our adopted home for underprivileged children.

As the night goes on, the noise gets louder, with laughter, jokes and general chit-chat. At about 2230, my mate Tony (one of the Chiefs from 800 Squadron. We served together on 800 Buccaneer Squadron from 1969 to 1972), thinks that it is a good idea to go and paint two whales on the scoreboard on the side of the island. So, we cut out the shape of a whale on a piece of A4 paper, go down to my workshop, put our overalls on, get some black paint and off we go up to the flight deck, like daft school kids, but we think more like SAS – stealth-like. The flight deck is in total darkness, so we creep around undetected. Fortunately, there is a permanent vertical ladder up the side of the island by the scoreboard, so the both of us climb up it. I hold the template in position while Tony applies the paint. On completion, we make a hasty retreat back to the workshop to remove our overalls. By the time we get back to the mess, we find the bar was closed, so we come up with another idea to get a final beer before calling it a day. "Let's go down to the Aft Warrant (Fleet Chief) officers and CPOs' mess," so off we go, making our way through the many passageways within the ship. On reaching the other mess, we ring the bell. Of all the people on the ship to answer the door, the bloody Jossman opens it. On seeing the two of with our hands covered in black paint, he asks: "What the f**k have you two been up to?" Then he adds: "I don't want to know." We have a beer and a chat with the guys there, then make our way to our cabins, all excited about tomorrow, and get our heads down after a great night.

The next day, up nice and early, as I go for breakfast, I notice in the pot wash that the picture diary is complete. It is amazing! The story of our last few months is now finished for everyone to see and remember, denoting everything that had happened. I wish that I had taken a photograph of it.

On the flight deck, everyone is getting prepared for the Prime Minister's arrival. The weather is perfect; nice and sunny and with everything on the flight deck in place. When she arrives by helicopter, the Captain and other high-ranking officers will be there to greet her, when she alights from the helicopter. When she does arrive and is getting out of the helicopter, she has the biggest smile on her face you can imagine; it stretches from ear to ear. They all leave the flight deck, no doubt to go and meet more of the officers and crew. I don't know how long she stayed but it wasn't long before she got back into the helicopter and was away.

The ship is now ready to weigh anchor, which will be about 1300-ish, so time for lunch and to get into our best uniforms, then another beer before lining the flight deck in Procedure Alpha.

When it is time to line the flight deck, two other Chiefs and I are still enjoying our beer, so we quickly finish them, straighten our ties, brush off our jackets, grab our caps and off we go up to the flight deck. To get there we have to make our way along the all too familiar passageways, where nothing is hidden. As mentioned previously, all the pipework and miles upon miles of electrical cables are on show throughout the ship, including the first aid posts where the Neil Robertson stretchers are stowed, and where, over the past months, the first aid teams closed up for hours on end, just waiting, not known what was going to happen, with their anti-flash gear on. Alongside the first aid posts are the red boxes that house the breathing apparatus (BA) for use if there is a fire, and also pieces of timber for the damage control teams, which would be used to shore up damage or holes in the side. These areas are positioned throughout the ship at all levels.

Just two more levels to climb before we reach the door on flight deck level that gives you access to the deck.

Once on deck, I think the whole of the ship's company and our passengers are there, and I remember thinking or saying to Tony and Jim, "Who's driving the bloody ship?" The only free space left to man the edge of the deck was down aft next to the flagpole where the White Ensign was fluttering in the breeze. The reason why these were the only free spaces is that, being aft of the island where the ship's funnel is directing its exhaust smoke, you got gassed from the fumes from the engine room, but who cares today? We are nearly home after months at sea. It could have been snowing, raining, gale force winds – anything – it wouldn't have mattered. We are all as happy as pigs in shit (a naval saying meaning 'I'm really happy and no bastard is going to spoil it!').

The anchor is lifted out of the deep English Channel and we start to move slowly. Being down aft, you see the water behind the ship starting to churn up as the large propellers start to rotate, pushing the ship, with all onboard, weighing 22,000 tons, slowly moving forward. The engineers in the engine and boiler rooms, carrying out their last instructions from the bridge, to bring the 'Happy H' home, after spending months down in the depths of this mighty vessel, throughout action stations, cruising stations, RAS manoeuvres, these guys shut in below the waterline, not knowing what's going on, are now on top. I remember speaking to one of them while down south and he said, "I would rather be down there than up top." I was the other way around. Mind you, he was an ex-submariner!

Now we are coming around from the back of the Isle of Wight. Southsea has come into view and all you can see is a sea of people all along the shoreline; thousands of people all waving small Union Jacks and banners. Then small motorboats started to appear; motorboats from the dockyard keeping other vessels out of the way of this mighty, tired, battle-scarred, rusty, dirty, oil-stained warship, giving us a clear passage into the dockyard, and home.

Feelings and emotions on the ship are running high. The stress and adrenaline have gone. It is now history and memories. Memories of your shipmates who are not coming home, who are still on patrol and will be forever. What are the families thinking at the moment, seeing the homecoming of these ships being shown on the television? It must have been a tremendous heartache for them – the mums, dads, grannies, grandads, wives, sons, daughters, brothers and sisters. You can't imagine what they are going through; it must be terrible for them.

Every minute is bringing us closer to the dockyard. People everywhere. The Round Tower is getting closer, just before the entrance to the dockyard on the right. A small motorboat comes into view from alongside the ship. It stands out from all the others. Everyone onboard is cheering and focusing on this one boat. On closer inspection (well maybe 100 yards away), it is apparent that one of the ladies on the boat doesn't have her top on. What a homecoming! We all give her a wave. If ever that lady reads this, here is a big thank you!

As we enter the narrow gap, which is the entrance into the dockyard, over the ship's tannoy we hear, "Flight Deck ho" (the instruction "ho" in the Royal Navy means come to attention). HMS *Dolphin*, the Captain of the *Dolphin* and our Captain, Linley Middleton, exchange salutes, which lasts a good few seconds, then we get "Flight deck stand easy". HMS *Dolphin* is the Royal Navy's submarine base and training school and has a landmark: a 160-feet-tall building. This is the escape training tank, where the submariners learn how to escape from submerged submarines that are damaged or are in difficulties. Again, along the edge of *Dolphin*, there are people everywhere: on the sea wall, hanging out of windows, waving and cheering. Everywhere you look there are people. I think, who's doing the work now because it looks like everyone in the UK is here!

We are now getting closer to our berth – the final manoeuvre of the old lady. The tugs to assist us had joined us earlier to help us through the narrow gap and now push us alongside. It was at about this time that there was a flypast of our historic Swordfish aircraft, along with some others. Everyone onboard is now feeling like a celebrity. All these people have come to see us and no one else. It doesn't matter what ship you were on, they have all come to welcome us home after doing our duty 8,000 miles away.

Now we are within touching distance, within reach of land.

The tugs push the ship slowly towards the quay. Once close enough, the heaving lines are thrown ashore with precision and skill – something that hasn't been done for months, but it is done with perfection as always. Attached to the heaving lines are the main securing lines. The dockyard workers grab the heaving lines, pull the main securing lines ashore and slip them over the bollards along the quayside, attaching the ship to exactly the same position it left all those months ago, on 5 April; at that time none of us knowing what lay ahead.

While all this is going on, on the quay it is heaving with family and friends of everyone onboard the *Hermes*. They have had special permission to enter the dockyard for this very special occasion. They see the tattered old ship, that has probably been on the news since it left in April, exhausted from its tasks, just like the guys onboard. This ship is the largest ship in the Royal Navy, which, having been launched in the 1950s, has earned another battle honour, having proved to still be able to cope with anything thrown at it and its crew. It has performed better than the newer aircraft carriers that had trouble with vibration and speed and couldn't carry as many aircraft, although we still couldn't have done it without the *Invincible*. Invincible by name, invincible by nature. Well done. You'll soon be on your way home.

"Flight deck ho" and then "Flight deck dismiss" are announced, which means that we are now alongside. Everyone now rushes to the starboard side to look down at the mass of people on the quay, to see if they can recognise their wife, children, mum, dad; anyone they might know. There are flags flying and being waved from side to side, posters with messages on them: 'Welcome home Dad', 'Welcome home lads', 'Good old Hermes', 'Well done the Royal Marines' (the Royal Marines had the best position on the flight deck, overlooking the starboard side. Their bar must have been closed.)

Everyone is now waving and shouting at each other. Once they recognise someone below, you can see tears of happiness and joy on their faces, the odd one or two with hankies in their hands, wiping away the tears from their cheeks. The crew are now just waiting on the gangways to be attached; one forward and one aft for the officers. I look to see if I know anyone and then, with excitement and through tear-glazed eyes, I see my lovely kids holding a large banner reading 'Welcome home Dad'. Alongside them is their mother, who I divorced while I was away. The kids are waving madly and are jumping up and down. Then, not far from them, I see my sisters and their husbands, who must have arrived in Portsmouth the night before.

The atmosphere is now electric. The guys just want to get their feet on dry land and hug their loved ones, who they have missed so much. The day has been perfect in all respects: lovely sunny weather, seeing your family and friends, knowing you have arrived home safely after being to war and back. What more could you ask for?

A couple of people at a time start moving from the flight deck and make their way to where the gangways are, hoping to be one of the first to get ashore, but, when they get there, they find out that hundreds of others have had the same idea, so they join the queue and just wait. Well, what's a couple more minutes' wait going to matter after so long?

Back on the flight deck and weather deck, those that aren't in the queue to go ashore are still looking for their families and loved ones, or are looking to see if they recognise anyone. When people seen anyone they know, they start shouting and cheering and waving so that they can be recognised, but I'm sure that from the quay looking up everyone looked the same! To get the attention of someone on the quay that they know, some of the guys are throwing their caps into the crowd. I don't think they ever saw them again!

Both gangways are now in position. I notice that at the bottom of each gangway there are two people giving everyone that goes ashore a red rose; a lovely touch. The Royal Marine band is still playing; they are the best military band in the world. The whole atmosphere is really emotional. There is now a steady stream of men coming off both gangways; all of them with the biggest grins on their faces. They are now on dry land at exactly the same spot they had left to board the ship that took them to war. You can see the relief on their faces, as they hit terra firma, looking for those they have missed and have been writing to over the past months, sharing their experiences by letter. There are lots of hugs going on on the quay, tears flowing, lots of kissing and lots of relief that we are home, but not forgetting our chums on other ships who didn't come home. We'll never forget them. But, the happiness and joy all along the jetty is an experience that you will never have again.

I have attempted to put all of this into words. It is difficult to explain what creates the relief of being home. Especially this trip, which wasn't like any other; it was one that I don't think anyone will want to repeat.

I eventually get my feet on the gangway, knowing that the other end is on dry land. What a feeling! I'm nearly there! What am I going to expect? I'm no longer married but I do have my lovely kids. As I'm about halfway down, faces start to become familiar, then I see a banner which, like all the others, is home made from bedsheets, paper and cardboard. The banner I instantly recognise. I know it is for me; not because it has my name on it or welcome home dad, but because it is being held up by my two great kids, with huge smiles on their faces, with their mother standing next to them.

Arriving at Portsmouth, 1982.

I get to the bottom of the gangway and am given my red rose. The person handing it to me says, "Welcome home, Jack, and well done." I am making my way over to the kids, when I notice my sisters and their husbands there also. Tears of joy and relief start to flow. I get to the kids and just hug them, thinking to myself that, no matter what, I'm never going to abandon them and am going to make sure they are looked after.

Tremendous welcome returning to Portsmouth, 1982.

Coming ashore.

Slowly, very slowly, everyone starts to disperse from the jetty, still with their banners and small Union Jacks held aloft. Everyone is simply enjoying the moment; a moment and an experience we did not expect. We were just doing our job, that we, the British military, had been trained for. I couldn't praise my team enough. Their average age was probably 21 or 22. They returned as men, and I felt responsible for their safety, although, on the other hand, they had also watched out for me when we were on the flight deck and everything was happening and you needed eyes in the back of your head. Harriers landing behind you! Taking cover in the catwalks by the ammunitions dump! These lads were also the eyes in the back of my head.

Now that we are back home, I hope that the people on the Falklands appreciate what we did and the sacrifices made. We are now in among our families and friends and the questions start: "What was it like?" "Where were you?" "Did you see any action?" "Were you frightened?" I still get asked these questions today and all of it comes flooding back as if it was only yesterday.

We are home now, and life must go on. I'll be back onboard later to carry on with my tasks, preparing my department and getting it ready for going back to sea.

CHAPTER FOURTEEN

Life goes on

~ • ~

So, the next few weeks are going to be just as busy, offloading the unserviceable aircraft engines, rotor blades from the helicopters, gearboxes, etc. The day after we return, one of MARTSU's lorries arrives to collect the unserviceable engines. I recognise the driver; it was 'old Jack', an ex-Royal Navy stocker from World War II. When he gets onboard, I ask him if he wants a drink. "Tea, coffee, Jack?" "No," he replies, "I'd like a drink." it was only 0930, so off to my cabin we go and he drinks nearly three-quarters of a bottle of my precious rum!

Everything onboard now is being done at a slower pace, taking time to stop whatever you are doing to have a chat with anyone who wants to talk.

The squadron personnel and the Royal Marines had all disembarked back to their parent air stations, so the ship was now manned totally by the ship's company; the majority of whom had now gone on well-deserved leave to recuperate and rest (well, get pissed and party, which they all deserved). It will take a while for the crew to adjust back to normality. I now have to get the vehicles ashore: the Captain's Land Rover and the flight deck tractors to the MOD garage for servicing and repair. The same with all the other vehicles

The dockyard workers are now back onboard – there are green overalls moving about all over the ship – carrying their toolboxes with them, along with pieces of equipment that have either been removed or are going to be fitted, just like during the days before we sailed for the South Atlantic.

Now that we were back, because the ship had been on food rationing from the day we departed until we reached Ascension on our way home, the caterers needed to catch up on the money they had to spend; otherwise their budget for the following year would have been affected (cut), so, for lunch for a week or so we ate like royalty. Fillet steaks, T- bone steaks, smoked salmon, prawns, etc. The lunch hour seemed to extend a bit longer every day. Still, no one really cared. We just enjoyed it while it lasted because, like everything else, all good things come to an end at some time.

That year, 1982, the ship didn't open to the public during Navy Days because it wasn't ready for visitors; it was too dangerous to allow them onboard. I knew that the visitors would require ice cream, so I managed to obtain a 'chacon' (a small container), placed it on the jetty next to the gangway, ran an electrical cable from the ship to power the freezers, and stocked them with ice cream. I also had a stock of T-shirts with pictures of the ship on the front. Everything sold like hot cakes; everyone wanted mementoes. However, it wasn't all plain sailing because the civilians who had their stalls in the dockyard for the open days complained about ours, which seemed to please the guys on the ship. We just carried on as usual.

As for me, I'm still confused, but I'm home now with my children, not knowing what the future holds for me with my family. Only time will tell. I only hope that I don't cause them anymore heartache. I'll just have to take each day as it comes.

CHAPTER FIFTEEN

Return to the Falklands

~ • ~

The year is now 2016; 34 years since the conflict. Last year, I noticed a cruise advert. It was for 54 days, leaving the UK on 5 January, visiting several places: Brazil, Uruguay, Chile, Argentina and the Falkland Islands. So I thought, I must go on this cruise. I need to find out if it had been worth it – all those lives lost on both sides – which has been on my mind all these years. The *Belgrano* sinking, those poor sailors in the freezing water and the ones that didn't survive. Our lads caught up with trying to save their ship after being hit and the acts of bravery that weren't recorded: shipmates trying to save each other, trying to extinguish fires, knowing that it is impossible. Just doing their job, if you ever ask them.

I really didn't know what to expect when I got there. On the way down, prior to reaching the islands, a service was held onboard as we passed the entrance to the River Plate, to remember the sailors lost in action during the Battle of the River Plate. Another service was held the night before we arrived in the Falklands. Both services were very emotional and were well attended by passengers and crew. It is at times like these that the memories come flooding back, as if it was yesterday. Also, it reminded me of the memorial service that was held on the flight deck of the *Hermes* at Ascension Island on our way home. In your head, you see all your pals and shipmates as you remember them. 'They Shall Not Grow Old as You Grow Old.'

We arrive in Port William (although, according to Google Maps, it's now called Blanco Bay. Also, next to where it mentions the Falkland Islands, in brackets it reads 'Islas Malvinas'. This must really annoy the locals.)

Port William is a bay just outside the entrance into Port Stanley. As soon as I knew that the Falklands were in sight, I was up on deck; I didn't want to miss anything. As we slowly made our way into Port William's anchorage, I could see the same little houses that I had seen 34 years ago, all looking the same from a distance. Eventually, I could hear the anchor

AED Department H.M.S. Hermes.

chain being let out, and realised that we were anchoring in more or less the exact same position as the *Hermes* had anchored all those years ago. I could see in my mind's eye the helicopters' flypast over Stanley, with one of the helicopters flying the White Ensign, fluttering in the downdraft of the rotor blades. The Royal Navy had won another battle honour, albeit at the expense of so many ships. It was a funny feeling now, not knowing what to expect or what the reaction would be when I spoke to the inhabitants on the island.

My wife and I managed to get on the first boat going ashore, along with a member of the Royal British Legion (RBL) and his wife, and an ex-RAF regiment guy and his wife, who asked me if I would lay a wreath that he had been given from a relative of a Welch Guard who never came home. I felt really privileged and honoured to be able to carry out this task.

When we arrived ashore, we were met by members of the local RBL. Prior to leaving Southampton, I had been in touch with the South Atlantic Medal Association 82 (SAMA 82), who had put me in touch with the lady who runs Liberty Lodge: a lodge that provides accommodation for veterans of the 1982 conflict. I looked around the landing area to see if anyone was holding a sign with my name on it, but couldn't see anyone. There were lots of tour guides there, waiting to take people to see the penguins and other places of interest, so my wife and I tagged along with the others.

The two guys who met us were both ex-Royal Navy. One of them, John, was a retired submariner, a Lieutenant Commander, and the other an ex-FAA PO handler. Both of them had relocated to the Falklands a few years previously. Once we had had coffee, introduced ourselves and had some photos taken, they took us around the Stanley area in their vehicles to visit sites that would be of interest to us. Barry, the chap that was with us from the RBL, had brought their branch's 'Standard' with him, wanting to have it photographed at some of the memorials that had been erected around Stanley.

One of the first stops was the cenotaph, overlooking the bay of Port Stanley, followed by a visit to the cemetery, situated next to the cenotaph. It's not until you visit places like these that you realise how cruel life can be, cutting short the lives of both young and old sailors. There were many

Receiving Captain's Prize, 1982.

graves of the sailors who paid the ultimate sacrifice, after being involved in action far from home. I was now thinking, should I have come here? We then took a short walk up the hill and into Memorial Wood, where a tree had been planted in memory of all the British servicemen who had lost their lives during the 1982 conflict. There was a map near the entrance informing you of where the trees were and who they were planted for. I looked for the names of two guys I had served with, back in the 1970s. I looked for their trees and, after a little searching, found them. The memories once again came flooding back; not just of the times we worked together but I also started to try and imagine what they must have suffered, although I hoped and prayed that they hadn't suffered. My emotions started getting the better of me and I just stood there thinking, was all this worth it? Seeing all those trees, each one someone's husband, son, friend, etc., I'm sure that all of it could have been avoided. If the politicians had done their job properly, this wood wouldn't be here and these poor guys would have had a longer life. One of the guys escorting us came and asked me if I was alright. I must admit it was hard for me to hold back the tears and take it all in.

On the *Hermes*, we only knew what was going on ashore and on the ships close to land from the news reports that came over the radio, or news of battle progress from the ship's bridge, usually from our own Captain. It

View into hangar down south, 1982.

took me a few minutes to reflect and absorb what had actually happened all those years ago, and trying to understand why. I still can't answer that question and convince myself that it had all been worth it. We spent about 30 minutes within the wood, which is looked after and attended to by the local cadet force. On behalf of all of us, a big thank you.

We left there, my eyes still full of tears, but keeping my thoughts to myself, and made our way back to the transport. As we drove along Sea Road, we passed Liberty Lodge on our left. I remember thinking, what a lovely-looking building. It looked really welcoming but, unfortunately, we didn't have time to stop. I would have liked to have met up with the people who ran it and the veterans who visited the islands.

The next stage of the visit was a bit of a touristy thing. We visited an area where there were some penguins on the beach. Unfortunately, we couldn't get closer to them because of some fenced-off areas where there was the possibility of landmines still being there since the conflict. I have often wondered if the Argentinians had a map showing where the mines had been positioned, or did they know that they weren't going to win, so they didn't bother mapping them out. The mind boggles.

I'm glad that I made the effort and visited the islands. It was very emotional for me but worth it, seeing them in their rugged splendour. At sea, we could only imagine what they were like. After sailors have been at sea for so long, seeing land reminds you that you are not alone on this planet, reminding you that others share this wonderful place called earth. It is just annoying that there are people on earth who want more than their fair share, which causes conflicts throughout the world, where innocent people get involved and are killed trying to protect their little 'patch'.

RIP all those on both sides who never returned home, and all those who have 'crossed the bar since and remain on patrol forever'.

There were no awards given to any of the ship's company of the *Hermes*, although I was informed by Whato (my boss, Lt Whiting) that I had been put forward for one, but we all deserved one. We were a team – a family – manning one of the Royal Navy's greatest ships ever during a time of war. I believe that there were awards given to others back home who did their bit and were home every night, but that's 'life in a blue suit.'

My story is dedicated to Dave and Allan and **all** who paid the ultimate sacrifice, who will never grow old, like me, who has grown old. I still see them as young men of the 1970s and 1980s.

These young men gave the Falkland Islands and their inhabitants their 'freedom from the sea'.

Lt. Chas Chambers and myself relaxed from action stations.

Glossary

~ • ~

ACR	Aircraft Control Room
ACRB	aircrew refreshments
ACRO	Aircraft Control Room Officer
AED	Aircraft Engineering Department
AEO	Aircraft Engineering Officer
AMCO	Aircraft Maintenance Control Office
BA	breathing apparatus
CAP	carrier aircraft patrol
CASVACS	casualty evacuations
CPO	Chief Petty Officer
FAA	Fleet Air Arm
FDO	Flight Deck Officer
FFO	furnace fuel oil
Flyco	flying operations control from here
FOB	Forward Operation Base
GMT	Greenwich Mean Time
HIFR	helicopter inflight refuelling rig
MARTSU	mobile aircraft repair and transport salvage unit
ORI	operational readiness inspection
RAS	replenishment at sea
RBL	Royal British Legion
RFA	Royal Fleet Auxiliary
RNAS	Royal Naval Air Station

RPO	Regulating Petty Officer
SAMA 82	South Atlantic Medal Association 82
SAS	Special Air Service
SBS	Special Boat Service
SMR	Senior Maintenance Rating
STUFT	ships taking up from trade
TEZ	Total Exclusion Zone
TWDTWGH	that will do till we get home

```
PVZCZCBWA32M   UU
OO RBDAPZ
DE RBDTWM 002 1563155
ZNR UUUUU
O 151127Z JUN 82
FM TPS HEREFORD
TO RBDEC/CTF 317
RBDFNR/CTG 317
RBDFNR/CTG 317.0
RBDICU/CTG 317.9
INFO RBDAPZ/CTU 317.1.1
RBDAPZ/CTU 317.1.2
BT
UNCLAS
SIC 19F
THE FOL IS THE TEXT OF A MSG FROM 317.1 PASSED VIA HEREFORD TO
ADDRESSEES ABOVE. MSG BEGINS.
HQ LFFI PORT STANLEY. IN PORT STANLEY AT 9 O'CLOCK PM FALKLAND
ISLANDS TIME TONIGHT THE 14 JUN 1982, MAJOR GENERAL MENENDES
SURRENDERED TO ME ALL THE ARGENTINE ARMED FORCES IN EAST AND WEST
FALKLAND, TOGETHER WITH THEIR IMPEDIMENTA. ARRANGEMENTS ARE IN
HAND TO ASSEMBLE THE MEN FOR RETURN TO ARGENTINA, TO GATHER IN
THEIR ARMS AND EQUIPMENT, AND TO MARK AND MAKE SAFE THEIR MUNITIONS.
THE FALKLAND ISLANDS ARE ONCE MORE UNDER THE GOVERNMENT DESIRED

PAGE 2 RBDTWM 002 UNCLAS
BY THEIR INHABITANTS.
GOD SAVE THE QUEEN.
SIGNED JJ MOORE.
MSG ENDS
BT
```

The surrender document.

CPSIA information can be obtained
at www.ICGtesting.com
Printed in the USA
BVHW071154301020
592212BV00011B/895

9 781527 248236